Diabetic Diet

After 50

Ultimate Low-Carb, Low-Sugar Recipe Book with Over 2000+ Days of Recipes for Longevity Beyond 50 & 30-Day Detox Plan + Exclusive Medical Consultation Included.

Dr. Madison Wells

Table Of Content :

Introduction

The Importance of a Diabetic Diet After 50

Embarking on the second half-century of life brings its own set of challenges and opportunities, especially when it comes to health. For those among us navigating the complexities of managing diabetes after the age of fifty, understanding the critical role of diet can turn the tide from merely surviving to thriving.

Why Focus on Diet at This Stage?

As we age, our bodies undergo significant changes that can impact how we process food, with metabolism slowing down and the risk for chronic diseases like diabetes increasing. Managing diabetes effectively requires a proactive approach, one where diet plays a central role. But this isn't just about controlling diabetes; it's about redefining what our later years look like.

A well-crafted diabetic diet after 50 doesn't just aim to keep blood sugar levels in check. It's about nurturing the body, energizing it, and ensuring that each meal brings not just nutritional value but joy and satisfaction. At this stage, our dietary choices can dramatically affect our quality of life, influencing everything from our weight to our energy levels and even our emotional well-being.

Food as Medicine

Think of your diet as your daily dose of medicine—one that tastes good, fuels your body, and brings you happiness. A diabetic diet tailored for those over fifty takes into account the unique nutritional needs of aging adults. It emphasizes foods that are rich in nutrients, low in unhealthy fats and simple sugars, but high in fiber. These elements are essential not only for managing blood glucose levels but for supporting heart health, preserving muscle mass, and ensuring that your body gets a full range of vitamins and minerals necessary for optimal health.

Tailoring to Taste and Tradition

One of the beautiful aspects of focusing on diet is the ability to customize it to fit personal tastes, cultural traditions, and social occasions. This book is not about giving you a one-size-fits-all solution but rather providing the tools to tailor your dietary approach to suit your preferences. Whether it's adapting traditional recipes to make them more diabetes-friendly or finding ways to enjoy social gatherings without compromising your health goals, there's room for flexibility and creativity.

Adopting a diabetic diet isn't about restrictions; it's about making smart choices that enhance your life. It's possible to enjoy a rich, varied diet that satisfies not only your nutritional needs but also your soul's craving for delicious, comforting food.

Breaking the Cycle of Fear with Knowledge and Choice

Many approach diet changes with trepidation, fearing the loss of favorite foods or the imposition of a bland, unsatisfying menu. However, armed with the right knowledge and practical strategies, you can craft a way of eating that is both health-promoting and deeply satisfying. Understanding how different foods affect your blood sugar and learning how to balance meals can transform your relationship with food. It's about gaining control over your diabetes, rather than letting it control you.

This book aims to demystify the diabetic diet for those over fifty, providing clear, easy-to-follow guidance that's rooted in the latest science yet personalized to fit your lifestyle.

By embracing this approach, you're not just managing diabetes; you're setting the stage for a healthier, happier, and more vibrant life as you age.

A Call to Action

If you're reading this, you're already taking the first step towards a healthier future. With each page turn, you'll find not just recipes and dietary advice but a new perspective on what it means to live well with diabetes after 50. This is more than a diet; it's a lifestyle choice that empowers you to take control of your health, one meal at a time.

How This Book Can Help You Achieve a Healthier Lifestyle

Tailoring Nutrition to Our Silver Years

To live healthily, actively, and independently for as long as possible without becoming a burden to our loved ones is a common and attainable dream. However, the fear of health complications often looms large, sending many in search of reliable information and tools. This book exists to dissolve those fears, serving up a feast of knowledge tailored to your needs.

Nutrition is not a one-way street; it is a complex network, and this book maps it out for you. Here you will learn how to manage health through a specific diet designed for your unique body and circumstances. The wisdom within these pages does not choke your lifestyle with intimidating restrictions but widens your culinary horizon, turning potential limitations into exploratory opportunity.

Practical Wisdom for Long-Term Wellness

The main premise underpinning this volume is the idea of practical implementation. You won't find excessively flowery language or bewildering medical jargon here. The goal is to walk you through, step by step, making sense of complex concepts in an accessible manner.

We will delve into how to build and sustain healthy habits that are enjoyable over time, thus nullifying the fear that a diabetes diagnosis means a constrained life. Crafting a healthy plate becomes an act of empowerment, not a chore. This book teaches you to embrace good food choices as part of a wider holistic approach without ever feeling deprived.

A Fresh Perspective on Managing Diabetes

Throughout this text, you'll find a fresh perspective on what it means to live with diabetes. There's an emphasis on creativity within your diet, enabling you to discover new, tasty recipes that abide by your nutritional requirements. We confront the stereotype that healthy food is bland head-on, showcasing how a diet rich in variety is within arm's reach.

This approachable playbook equips you with the means to turn everyday meals into therapeutic triumphs. Your culinary routine no longer revolves around diabetes; diabetes adapts to your routine. By taking control of your mealtime, you reclaim much more than your palate—you regain your health and zest for life.

Introducing Lifelong Independence Through Diet

In these pages, you'll find no quick fixes or fad diets. Instead, it's about introducing and maintaining a way of eating that brings you closer to lifelong independence. Whether it's understanding the glycemic index of your favorite apple variety or reimagining your family's treasured spaghetti recipe, we've got you covered.

The recipes and strategies within these pages help foster a sense of control over your health. They're developed with your active life in mind, designed to fit around your schedule, your social life, and your personal taste preferences.

Empowerment Through Education

Each page aims to educate, not intimidate. The more you know about how your body interacts with the foods you love, the more empowered you become to make the best choices for your health. This book does not confine or limit; it liberates, providing you with the confidence needed to craft daily meals that satisfy both your nutritional needs and your love of eating.

Conclusion

In essence, this book is a testament to the power of proactive health management through diet, especially after the age of fifty. It's a practical tool, packed with the advice, guidance, and recipes you need to live robustly despite diabetes. By the end of this book, you'll have not just a series of meals to prepare but a new outlook on life with diabetes, one that sees each sunrise not as a challenge but as an opportunity to thrive.

Success Stories from People Over 50 Who Have Adopted This Approach

Success Stories from People Over 50 Who Have Adopted This Approach

The golden years can usher in their own set of challenges, particularly for those managing diabetes. It's a time when the vigor of health becomes paramount, yet the path to achieving it can seem labyrinthine. However, the many individuals who have seamlessly blended the principles outlined in this book into their lives stand as living testimonies to the potency of a tailored diabetic diet after 50. Their stories are not just narratives of overcoming but are beacons of hope for others who might feel disheartened in their journey toward a healthier life.

Transformations Through Dietary Adaptation

Meet James, a 65-year-old retiree, who had struggled with yo-yo dieting for years. The onset of Type 2 diabetes was a wake-up call that forced him to rethink his approach to health. After adopting the low-carb and low-sugar diet principles as detailed in our guide, James found his glucose levels stabilizing. What was more remarkable, according to him, was the influx of energy he experienced—energy that had seemed to ebb away with age. With an attentive palate, James discovered the nuances of flavor in whole foods, savoring the sweetness of a ripe strawberry, the earthiness of almonds, and the zing of fresh herbs.

Then there's Linda, who at 58, feared that her diagnosis spelled the end of culinary delights. She loved to cook and share meals with her large family, and the thought of bland, uninspiring dishes was disheartening. By integrating the rich array of recipes provided in this book—each punctilious in its balance of nutrition without compromising taste—Linda found herself reinvigorated. Her kitchen buzzed with activity, her family gatherings grew even more joyful, and Linda, in control of her diabetes, became an advocate for a healthful lifestyle in her community.

Overcoming Challenges with Creativity

The beauty of adapting to a lifestyle conscious of diabetes lies in the way it requires creativity. Consider the story of Roberto, a seasoned food critic, who learned at 54 that his blood sugar levels were higher than they should be. For someone who savored every nuance of flavor, the dietary restrictions threatened the very essence of his trade. Yet, Roberto saw it not as a limitation but as an invitation to explore. He took to the kitchen, guided by the principles laid out within these pages, challenging himself to re-invent classic dishes in a manner that was both healthy and hearty. His column soon took on a new life, as he shared his journey and recipes that impressed even the most discerning palates.

Empowerment Through Education

Education, as echoed in the stories of those like Maria, is the cornerstone of empowerment. After her diagnosis at age 51, Maria felt swamped by a sea of misinformation. This book served as her lighthouse, steering her toward sound nutritional choices. With easy-to-understand explanations and actionable advice, Maria felt capable of managing her meals in a way that restored her confidence. Her success was not just in the numbers that reflected better glycemic control, but in the spirited approach she adopted toward diet, viewing each meal as an opportunity to nourish both body and soul.

Conclusion: A Chorus of Triumph

As these stories illustrate, the journey to a healthier lifestyle post-50, while nuanced with individual challenges, resonates with a universal chorus of triumph. The voices of those who rewrote their stories with the guidance of a diabetes-tailored diet echo with vivacity, inviting others to join in their vibrancy. Their experiences, while unique, serve as exuberant affirmations that a life well-lived, a life of health, active participation, and independence, is accessible to all who choose this path. It underscores the power situated within informed choices, mindful eating, and the joyous rediscovery of food's true purpose: sustenance, pleasure, and connection.

BONUS

We understand the critical role of tailored medical advice in navigating the complexities of diabetes, especially as dietary needs and health considerations become more nuanced with age. Therefore, as a complement to the wealth of knowledge you'll gain here, you'll have the unique opportunity to download "***The Complete Diabetic Dessert Almanac: Sweet Freedom from A to Z***" entirely free of charge by scanning the QR code provided.

Moreover, this comprehensive approach to managing your condition is further enriched with an "***Exclusive Medical Consultation via Email with Dr. Madison Wells***." This unique opportunity allows you to engage directly with me, to ask for more information, and personalized suggestions.

The almanac of desserts, paired with the prospect of an exclusive consultation, transforms this book from a mere guide into a holistic resource that empowers you to take joyous control over your dietary choices and overall health.

Scan the QR code and embrace these additional tools designed to complement and complete the valuable insights you hold in your hands.

Chapter 1:

The Link Between Diabetes and Age

1.1 Age-Related Risk Factors

Age-Related Risk Factors

As we navigate the voyage beyond 50, our physical constitution encounters a myriad of changes, some subtle and others more pronounced. Among these, the risk of developing diabetes or the challenge of managing pre-existing diabetes looms significantly larger. Understanding age-related risk factors is pivotal in harnessing control over diabetes and embracing a healthier lifestyle.

As we age, our bodies undergo natural physiological shifts that can increase our susceptibility to diabetes. A decrease in muscle mass and a consequential rise in body fat percentage alter the way our bodies process sugars, often leading to insulin resistance, a precursor to Type 2 diabetes. Moreover, pancreatic function, responsible for insulin production, can wane with age, complicating glucose management.

Another factor is the tendency for physical activity levels to drop as we grow older. Sedentary lifestyles contribute to obesity, a key risk factor for diabetes. Coupled with a natural decline in metabolic rate, the stage is set for the onset or worsening of diabetic conditions.

Hormonal changes also play a role. For women, the transition through menopause can lead to an increased risk due to changes in hormone levels that can affect insulin sensitivity. For men, a decrease in testosterone levels has been linked to reduced muscle mass and increased body fat, contributing further to insulin resistance.

The genetic predisposition towards diabetes doesn't diminish with age. If anything, years of accumulated stress, dietary habits, and environmental factors can activate these genetic markers, escalating the risk.

Unique Challenges for Those Over 50 with Diabetes

Managing diabetes post-50 presents a set of unique challenges that call for specific strategic approaches. One of the foremost challenges is the balancing act between managing diabetes and other age-related health conditions. High blood pressure, cholesterol issues, and heart disease often go hand-in-hand, necessitating a comprehensive approach to wellness that encompasses all facets of health.

Another significant challenge is the slower healing process in older adults, which can make managing the side effects of diabetes, such as wounds and sores, particularly problematic. This underscores the importance of proactive health management to prevent complications.

Furthermore, dietary management can be more complex due to changes in appetite and digestive processes that occur with age. The body's ability to assimilate nutrients changes, making it crucial for dietary plans to be adaptable and rich in essential nutrients. Understanding these physiological shifts is paramount in creating a sustainable and effective dietary regimen.

Medication management also becomes more intricate with age. The interactions between diabetes medication and drugs for other age-related conditions must be carefully considered, requiring a well-coordinated effort between healthcare providers and the individual.

Debunking Myths About Diabetes and Aging

One common misconception is the belief that diabetes is an inevitable part of aging. While risk factors increase with age, diabetes is not a foregone conclusion. Through diet, exercise, and mindful health practices, managing or even preventing diabetes is a feasible objective.

Another myth is the notion that seniors with diabetes cannot enjoy food. The reality, however, is quite the opposite. A well-structured diabetic diet can be both nutritious and full of flavors, turning meal times into delightful, healthful experiences rather than restrictive routines.

In conclusion, understanding the intricate relationship between diabetes and age is fundamental. Recognizing the age-related risk factors, addressing the unique challenges, and debunking prevalent myths pave the way for a proactive approach to diabetes management. It highlights the importance of a tailored diabetic diet and lifestyle modifications that resonate with the needs of those aged 50 and beyond. With informed decisions and committed action, navigating the path to a healthier, vibrant life is not just possible; it's within reach.

1.2 Unique Challenges for Those Over 50 with Diabetes

Unique Challenges for Those Over 50 with Diabetes

As individuals cross the threshold of 50, managing diabetes morphs into a multifaceted endeavor, intertwining health maintenance with the pursuit of a fulfilling life. This demographic not only faces the universal challenges of diabetes management but also encounters unique obstacles dictated by the progression of age. Navigating these challenges with grace and efficiency is essential for maintaining health and vitality, allowing individuals to lead enriching lives without being overshadowed by their condition.

Coping with Coexisting Conditions

One of the paramount challenges for those over 50 is the management of other health conditions alongside diabetes. It's not uncommon for hypertension, cholesterol irregularities, and cardiovascular diseases to accompany diabetes, creating a complex health landscape to navigate. This necessitates a comprehensive and holistic approach to health, one that requires meticulous coordination with healthcare providers to ensure that treatments are harmonized, minimizing the risk of adverse interactions and maximizing overall well-being.

Mitigating Slowed Physical Recovery

Aging undeniably affects the body's recuperative powers. For those managing diabetes, this can translate into slower healing of wounds, a heightened risk of infections, and a prolonged recovery process from illnesses or surgeries. The implications of this are profound, as minor injuries can escalate into serious complications if not managed with care. It underscores the importance of vigilant self-care routines, regular monitoring of blood sugar levels, and adherence to a lifestyle that supports optimum immune function.

Dietary Dilemmas and Nutritional Nuances

As we age, our metabolism slows, our digestive system undergoes changes, and our sense of taste may evolve. For those over 50 with diabetes, these shifts present unique dietary challenges. Striking a balance between managing blood sugar levels and ensuring adequate nutritional intake becomes a fine art. It demands a deeper understanding of how the body's needs change with age and how a diabetes-friendly diet can cater to these evolving requirements without compromising the pleasure of eating. This involves not just choosing the right foods but understanding portion sizes, the timing of meals, and the impact of food on blood glucose levels, ensuring that the diet remains both palatable and healthful.

Navigating Medication Management

For many over 50, diabetes management often involves a regimen of medication that works in tandem with lifestyle changes. However, as the number of medications for various conditions grows, so does the risk of drug interactions. This calls for a vigilant approach to medication management, one that involves open lines of communication with healthcare providers and a commitment to understanding how different medications interact with each other. It's about ensuring that the benefits of each medication are maximized while the risks are minimized, all within the context of comprehensive diabetes care.

Sustaining Motivation and Mental Health

Beyond the physical aspects of diabetes management lies the psychological battlefield. Staying motivated, dealing with the fears of complications, and maintaining a positive outlook are crucial yet often overlooked aspects of managing diabetes. Age can bring with it a sense of resignation or a feeling that it's too late to make meaningful changes. However, the opposite is true. This stage of life offers an opportunity to redefine oneself, to build and reinforce healthy habits that can profoundly impact one's quality of life. It necessitates fostering resilience, seeking support from peers and professionals alike, and cultivating a mindset that views diabetes management not as a burden but as a pathway to a more healthful and energetic existence.

Conclusion

The journey of managing diabetes over the age of 50 is undeniably challenging, marked by unique hurdles that require attention, determination, and a proactive stance towards health. However, it is also an opportunity—a chance to embrace a lifestyle that prioritizes well-being, discovers the joys of a healthful diet, and celebrates the capacity for renewal at any age. By recognizing and addressing these unique challenges head-on, individuals can navigate their golden years with confidence, grace, and an unwavering commitment to living life to the fullest, diabetes notwithstanding.

1.3 Debunking Myths About Diabetes and Aging

Embarking on managing diabetes after the age of 50 can feel like navigating through a forest dense with myths and misconceptions. These myths not only muddy the waters but can also lead to feelings of discouragement or an unwillingness to pursue healthier lifestyle changes. It's essential to clear the air, debunking these myths with factual, straightforward information. This will empower you to take control of your health, armed with knowledge and the motivation to implement effective strategies without being hindered by misinformation.

Myth 1: Diagnosis After 50 Means It's Too Late to Make a Difference

One of the most pervasive myths is the notion that being diagnosed with diabetes later in life means little can be done to improve one's health or quality of life. This couldn't be further from the truth. While it's undeniable that earlier intervention can prevent or delay the onset of diabetes-related complications, significant health improvements can still be made at any age. Management strategies focusing on dietary changes, physical activity, and medication adherence can markedly enhance blood sugar control, reduce the risk of complications, and improve overall well-being.

Myth 2: Severe Dietary Restrictions Are the Only Solution

Another common misunderstanding is that living with diabetes necessitates a life of extreme dietary deprivation, especially concerning carbohydrates. While mindful carbohydrate intake is a component of effective diabetes management, it doesn't mean you must live in a world devoid of culinary joy. The reality is more nuanced and encouraging: it's about making informed choices, understanding the impact of different foods on blood sugar levels, and finding a balance that supports blood sugar control while still allowing for the enjoyment of a wide variety of foods. The focus should be on complex carbohydrates with a low glycemic index, moderation, and the incorporation of diverse foods to ensure nutritional needs are met without sacrificing flavor or the social joy of eating.

Myth 3: Exercise Poses Too Much Risk for Older Adults with Diabetes

Physical activity is often met with caution or outright avoidance due to fears of injury or exacerbating health issues. However, exercise is a cornerstone of diabetes management at any age, offering profound benefits in improving glucose control, enhancing cardiovascular health, and boosting mental well-being. The key is choosing activities that you enjoy and that match your fitness level, which can include a range of options from walking and swimming to gentle yoga or tai chi. With appropriate medical guidance, the right exercise plan can significantly contribute to your diabetes management plan without putting your health at risk.

Myth 4: Insulin Use Is a Sign of Personal Failure

For many, the need to start insulin therapy is seen as a final defeat—a sign that they have failed to manage their diabetes effectively. This belief is not only damaging but fundamentally incorrect. Diabetes is a progressive disease, and over time, many individuals require insulin to maintain blood glucose levels within the target range. The initiation of insulin therapy reflects the natural course of the disease and the body's changing needs, not a failure on the individual's part. Understanding and accepting insulin as a valuable tool in diabetes management can transform it from a feared last resort to an embraced component of comprehensive care.

Myth 5: Diabetes Is an Inevitable Part of Aging

Lastly, there's the fatalistic view that diabetes is just an unavoidable aspect of growing older. While it's true that the risk of developing type 2 diabetes increases with age, it's far from an inescapable fate. Lifestyle factors play a considerable role in the onset and management of diabetes. Through informed dietary choices, regular physical activity, and ongoing medical care, the development of diabetes can be prevented or delayed, and its impact significantly mitigated even after diagnosis.

In Conclusion

Understanding the truth behind these myths is the first step in taking control of your diabetes management after 50. It opens the door to a world where diabetes can be managed effectively without fear, unnecessary restrictions, or misconceptions dictating your decisions.

Chapter 2:

The Principles of a Low-Carb and Low-Sugar Diet

2.1 Benefits of a Low-Carb and Low-Sugar Diet

Navigating Toward a Healthier Horizon

Embarking on the path to a low-carb and low-sugar diet after reaching the age of 50 comes at a critical juncture in life. It is a time when the body's metabolism is changing, and the necessity for more mindful eating habits becomes apparent. This approach to eating is not merely a diet but a transformative journey towards longevity and vitality.

For individuals who have been diagnosed with or are at risk of developing diabetes, embracing a low-carb and low-sugar lifestyle marks a decisive step in regaining control of their health. The benefits of such a diet are extensive and touch on various aspects of well-being, from physical health to emotional balance, offering a robust framework for managing diabetes effectively.

The Glycemic Balance

One of the primary advantages of limiting carbohydrates and sugars in your diet is the stabilization of blood glucose levels. Carbohydrates, especially those of the refined variety, tend to spike blood sugar levels rapidly. This spike can lead to volatile energy levels and mood swings, not to mention the long-term complications associated with consistently high blood glucose levels. By focusing on foods with a low glycemic index, you're ensuring a steadier, more manageable blood sugar level throughout the day, minimizing the risk of hyperglycemia and its associated risks.

Weight Management and Cardiovascular Health

A low-carb and low-sugar diet inherently leans towards foods that are higher in protein and healthy fats, which can aid in weight loss or weight management — a critical component in managing diabetes and overall health. Weight loss, particularly in the abdominal area, can significantly reduce the risk of developing further health issues, such as cardiovascular diseases. Foods rich in omega-3 fatty acids, for example, support heart health by reducing triglyceride levels and blood pressure, showcasing how a thoughtfully considered diet goes beyond mere diabetes management.

Energy Levels and Mental Clarity

Dietary choices have a profound impact on our energy levels and cognitive functions. High-carb meals can lead to a cycle of spikes and crashes in energy, contributing to feelings of fatigue and decreased mental acuity. In contrast, a diet that prioritizes low-carb and low-sugar intake supports sustained energy release. This consistency helps maintain alertness and clarity, enhancing day-to-day living by improving focus and productivity, making every moment more enjoyable and fulfilling.

Inflammation: The Silent Antagonist

Chronic inflammation is often an unseen adversary, implicated in a host of health issues from heart disease to arthritis and even diabetes. The adoption of a low-carb and low-sugar diet naturally steers you toward anti-inflammatory foods, like leafy greens, nuts, and fatty fish. This change can help reduce systemic inflammation, alleviating some of the discomforts associated with inflammatory conditions, and possibly reducing the progression of diabetes-related complications.

A Gateway to Culinary Discovery

Contrary to the dreary prospect of dietary restrictions, embracing a low-carb and low-sugar lifestyle opens the door to a world of culinary exploration. It encourages the discovery of new flavors, ingredients, and methods of preparation, turning every meal into an opportunity for creativity and enjoyment. This diet champions the consumption of whole, unprocessed foods, which, beyond their health benefits, often taste better and are more satisfying. This approach fosters a deep, appreciative relationship with food, where each meal supports your health goals and delights your palate.

Fostering a Sustainable Future

The beauty of adopting a low-carb and low-sugar diet lies not just in its immediate health benefits but in its sustainability. It is a way of eating that can be adapted and maintained throughout one's life, offering a practical solution to managing diabetes and promoting overall health. This diet is not a temporary fix but a sustainable lifestyle change, one that emphasizes the importance of making informed, health-conscious choices without the feeling of sacrifice or loss.

In essence, the advantages of a low-carb and low-sugar diet are manifold and extend well beyond blood sugar control. They touch upon every aspect of one's life, offering a holistic approach to health that balances physical well-being with emotional and mental vitality. This diet, when embraced wholeheartedly, offers a path to a healthier, more active, and independent life, free from the constraints of diabetes and full of the pleasures that come from nourishing the body and mind correctly.

2.2 Foods to Include and Avoid

Embracing a low-carb and low-sugar diet, especially after the age of 50, is akin to curating an art collection; it's about selecting pieces that not only have intrinsic value but also work together to create a cohesive, life-enhancing display. As we delicately navigate through this new dietary landscape, the choices we make at the grocery store, the farmer's market, or even within our own pantries, become essential to managing diabetes and crafting a healthy, joyful life.

The Inclusivity of Whole Foods

The cornerstone of a low-carb and low-sugar diet is whole foods. These are the foods that come from the earth and sea, offering robust flavors and nutrients without the need for added sugars or refined carbohydrates. It's about celebrating the unadorned beauty of food in its most natural form. This includes a wide variety of vegetables, particularly leafy greens like spinach, kale, and Swiss chard. These green powerhouses are low in carbs yet rich in fiber, vitamins, minerals, and antioxidants, capable of supporting diverse internal systems and combating oxidative stress.

Proteins embody the structural backbone of this diet. Poultry, fish, and lean cuts of meat stand proud as excellent sources of high-quality protein. Regular consumption of seafood, particularly fatty fish like salmon, mackerel, and sardines, can contribute to heart health thanks to their high omega-3 content. Plant-based proteins also play a significant role here. Legumes, although to be moderated due to their carb content, nuts, seeds, and tofu present a bouquet of options for those who are vegetarian or simply diversifying their protein sources.

Healthy fats are prized possessions in this dietary approach. They serve not only as a source of sustained energy but also assist in absorbing fat-soluble vitamins and minerals. Avocados, olives, almonds, and walnuts, along with their respective oils, offer monounsaturated fats which can aid in managing cholesterol levels, while seeds like flax and chia provide valuable omega-3 fatty acids that contribute to overall heart health.

Steering Clear of Refined Realities

With every inclusion comes the mindful practice of exclusion. The primary elements we aim to avoid are those of refined nature — the sugars and processed carbs that create turbulence in our metabolic wellbeing. This means setting aside those white breads, pastas, pastries, and high-sugar cereals, which are akin to cluttered brush strokes on our dietary canvas. They disrupt our glycemic control, potentially spiking blood sugar levels and complicating the body's insulin response.

Additionally, one should limit the intake of high-carb starchy vegetables like potatoes, corn, and peas, as these can also raise blood sugar levels. While whole fruits are generally a healthy choice, those with diabetes should consume them with consideration due to their natural sugar content, focusing on lower glycemic options such as berries and paying attention to portion sizes.

Packaged and processed foods often contain hidden sugars and unhealthy fats, diluting the purity of our diet with unnecessary additives and preservatives. These should be consumed sparingly, if at all, as a principle of this dietary approach. Beverages, too, fall under scrutiny, with sugary drinks, including sodas and fruit juices, being replaced by water, herbal teas, and other low-calorie options.

Cultivating a Taste for the Untainted

The integration of whole, unprocessed foods into daily life brings richness to the diet. It's about developing a sensory affair with the various textures, colors, and flavors of these foods. Envision preparing a grilled salmon with a side of roasted Brussels sprouts, or a colorful salad tossed with mixed greens, cherry tomatoes, cucumbers, and a handful of vibrant berries, all dressed with a drizzle of extra-virgin olive oil and a squeeze of fresh lemon. Such meals delight the senses and nourish the body while aligning with our goal of managing diabetes and maintaining a robust, active lifestyle.

Achieving a dietary balance often requires education and experimentation. The process of identifying the foods to embrace and those to avoid is a personal journey, one that revolves around cultivating an understanding of how various foods interact with your body, particularly your blood sugar levels. It's about fine-tuning your consumption habits, listening to what your body is telling you after each meal, and adjusting accordingly without casting a shadow of deprivation on your culinary experiences.

This chapter is about fostering an environment, both internally and externally, that is conducive to healthy living. The included and excluded foods are not just lists to be memorized but reflections of a lifestyle choice that puts your health and joy of living at the forefront. The low-carb and low-sugar diet is not a restrictive regime but a discerning embrace of foods that speak to our bodies' needs without silencing the pleasure of eating.

2.3 Tailoring the Diet to Your Needs and Preferences

Embarking on a dietary change, especially one that's focused on managing diabetes post-50, is no insignificant task. While low-carb and low-sugar diets are powerful tools in stabilizing blood sugar and improving overall health, personal tailoring ensures that this way of eating fits seamlessly into your life, enhancing it rather than becoming a source of stress or monotony. This personalization is key, allowing you to enjoy your meals, feel satiated, and maintain this lifestyle for the long term, all while keeping your glycemic levels in check.

Understanding Your Unique Nutritional Requirements

The first step towards personalizing your diet is understanding your body's unique needs. Age, activity level, weight, health conditions, and even medications can influence your nutritional requirements. Consulting with a healthcare provider or a dietitian can provide you with a tailored calorie and macro count, ensuring that you are not just eating healthily but optimally for your individual situation.

This understanding extends to recognizing how your body responds to different foods. Some might find that certain low-carb vegetables or dairy products affect their blood sugar differently. Monitoring how foods impact your glycemic levels can help you make informed decisions about what to incorporate regularly into your diet.

Incorporating Preferences and Lifestyle Considerations

Adapting the diet to fit your taste preferences and lifestyle is equally important. If you have a penchant for Italian cuisine, you might explore low-carb alternatives to pasta, such as zoodles (zucchini noodles) or spaghetti squash. If you're someone who frequently eats out or travels, researching or planning ahead can provide options that won't derail your dietary goals. Similarly, if cooking every day isn't feasible, identifying quick, simple meals or considering batch cooking could be game-changers.

Your cultural background and food traditions also play a vital role. A diet that alienates you from your cultural identity is unsustainable. Instead, find ways to modify traditional dishes by substituting ingredients or changing cooking methods. For example, swapping white rice for cauliflower rice in a beloved family recipe can allow you to enjoy a taste of home without compromising your dietary goals.

Flexibility and Moderation

Flexibility within your diet is necessary. Rigidity can lead to burnout or feelings of deprivation, which might derail your efforts. Instead, adopt a flexible mindset. Occasions like birthdays or holidays might warrant slight deviations from your strict dietary pattern. On such occasions, moderation is key. Enjoying a small serving of a higher-carb dish or indulging in a piece of birthday cake should not be seen as a failure but rather a part of a balanced, enjoyable lifestyle. It's what you do consistently that counts, not the occasional deviation.

Making Room for New Favorites

Discovering new foods and recipes is a delightful aspect of tailoring your diet. The world of low-carb cooking is vast and vibrant, bursting with ideas that challenge the misconception that dietary restriction equals boring food. From almond flour pancakes to cauliflower-crust pizzas, there are countless recipes designed to cater to low-carb preferences without sacrificing flavor. Investing time in finding recipes that excite your taste buds can make this dietary transition not just painless but enjoyable.

Listening to Your Body

Finally, the most important aspect of tailoring your diet is listening to your body. Your body gives continuous feedback, not just through blood sugar levels, but through energy levels, hunger cues, and how you feel overall. If certain aspects of your diet aren't working for you, be willing to adjust. This journey is personal and ever-evolving. What works perfectly today might need tweaking tomorrow. Staying attuned to your body's signals and being open to change ensures that your diet remains beneficial and sustainable.

Conclusion

Tailoring your low-carb and low-sugar diet to your specific needs and preferences is not just about making eating enjoyable; it's a critical step in ensuring success. It involves understanding your unique health requirements, incorporating lifestyle considerations, exercising flexibility, discovering new favorites, and continuously listening to your body. This approach makes it possible to manage diabetes effectively while living a full, vibrant life. After all, a diet should fit into your life, not dictate it.

Chapter 3:

Energizing Breakfasts

Recipe 1: Coconut Yogurt Parfait

-

Preparation time = 10 minutes

-Ingredients = 1 cup unsweetened coconut yogurt | 1/4 cup granola (gluten-free) | 1/2 cup mixed berries | 1 tablespoon flaxseeds

-Servings = Serves 1

-Mode of cooking: No cooking required

-Procedure:
Start by layering half of the coconut yogurt in a serving glass or bowl. Add a layer of granola over it, followed by a layer of mixed berries. Repeat the layering with the remaining yogurt, granola, and berries. Sprinkle flaxseeds on the top to finish.

-Nutritional values: 350 calories | 12g protein | 18g fat| 40g carbohydrates

Recipe 2: Sweet Potato & Avocado Toast

-Preparation time = 15 minutes

-Ingredients = 1 large sweet potato | 1 ripe avocado | 2 teaspoons lemon juice | Salt to taste | 1/4 teaspoon chili flakes | 1 tablespoon pumpkin seeds

-Servings = Serves 2

-Mode of cooking: Oven & Assembling

-Procedure:
Preheat the oven to 400°F (200°C). Slice the sweet potato lengthwise into 1/4 inch slices and bake for about 10 minutes until soft. In a bowl, mash the avocado with lemon juice and salt. Spread this mashed avocado onto each sweet potato slice, then sprinkle with chili flakes and pumpkin seeds before serving.

-Nutritional values: 280 calories | 5g protein| 15g fat | 35g carbohydrates

Recipe 3: Quinoa Veggie Breakfast Bowl

-Preparation time = 20 minutes

-Ingredients = 1/2 cup cooked quinoa | 1/4 cup diced red bell pepper | 1/4 cup shredded kale | 1/4 cup cherry tomatoes, halved | 1 tablespoon olive oil | 1 teaspoon apple cider vinegar | Salt and pepper to taste

-Servings = Serves 1

-Mode of cooking: Stove & Mixing

-Procedure:
Heat olive oil in a pan and sauté red bell pepper until soft. Add kale and cook until wilted. Mix the cooked quinoa with sautéed veggies, cherry tomatoes, apple cider vinegar, salt, and pepper in a bowl. Serve warm for a nourishing start to the day.

-Nutritional values: 320 calories | 8g protein | 14g fat| 45g carbohydrates

Recipe 4: Berry-Oat Smoothie Bowl

-Preparation time = 10 minutes

-Ingredients = 1/2 cup rolled oats (gluten-free) | 1 cup almond milk | 1/2 banana | 1 cup mixed berries (fresh or frozen) | 1 tablespoon chia seeds | 1 tablespoon hemp hearts

-Servings = Serves 1

-Mode of cooking: Blender

-Procedure:
Blend rolled oats, almond milk, banana, and mixed berries until smooth. Pour the mixture into a bowl and top with chia seeds and hemp hearts. This makes a wholesome smoothie bowl perfect for an energy boost.

-Nutritional values: 400 calories | 15g protein| 12g fat| 66g carbohydrates

Recipe 5: Spinach & Mushroom Omelet

-Preparation time = 15 minutes

-Ingredients = 2 large eggs | 1/4 cup chopped spinach | 1/4 cup sliced mushrooms | 1 tablespoon olive oil | Salt and pepper to taste

-Servings = Serves 1

-Mode of cooking: Stove

-Procedure:
Beat the eggs with salt and pepper. In a skillet, cook mushrooms in olive oil until soft and golden. Add spinach and cook until wilted. Pour the eggs over the veggies and cook covered until the eggs are set. Fold the omelet in half and serve hot.

-Nutritional values: 300 calories | 20g protein| 22g fat| 4g carbohydrate

Recipe 6: Avocado Toast with Poached Egg

-Prep Time: 15 minutes

-Ingredients: 2 slices of whole grain bread | 1 ripe avocado | 2 eggs | 1 tablespoon of vinegar | Salt and pepper to taste | Sesame seeds for garnish

-Servings: Serves 2

-Cooking Method: Toaster & Boiling

-Procedure:
Toast the bread slices until they are crispy. Mash the avocado and spread it over the toasted bread. Bring water to a boil in a small pot and add vinegar. Gently break an egg into a small dish and then slide it into the boiling water. Cook for 3-4 minutes. Remove the egg with a slotted spoon and let it drain. Repeat with the second egg. Place a poached egg on each slice of avocado

toast. Season with salt, pepper, and sesame seeds.

-**Nutritional Values:** 350 calories | 14g protein | 20g fat | 30g carbohydrates

Recipe 7: Spinach and Mint Smoothie

-**Prep Time:** 5 minutes

-**Ingredients:** 1 cup of fresh spinach | 1/2 cup of fresh mint | 1 green apple | 1 banana | 1/2 cup of almond milk | 1 tablespoon of flax seeds

-**Servings:** Serves 1

-**Cooking Method:** Blender

-**Procedure:**
Combine spinach, mint, green apple pieces, banana, almond milk, and flax seeds in a blender. Blend until smooth. Serve immediately to enjoy the

maximum nutritional benefits and a refreshing taste.

-**Nutritional Values:** 280 calories | 5g protein | 4g fat | 57g carbohydrates

Recipe 8: Quinoa and Cucumber Salad

-**Prep Time:** 20 minutes

-**Ingredients:** 1/2 cup of quinoa | 1 cucumber | 1/2 cup of cherry tomatoes | 1/4 cup of black olives | 1/4 cup of chopped red onion | 2 tablespoons of olive oil | 1 tablespoon of lemon juice | Salt and pepper to taste

-**Servings:** Serves 2

-**Cooking Method:** Boiling & Mixing

-**Procedure:**
Cook the quinoa as instructed on the package and let it cool. Dice the

cucumber, halve the cherry tomatoes, and chop the red onion. In a large bowl, combine cooled quinoa, cucumber, cherry tomatoes, olives, and red onion. Dress with olive oil, lemon juice, salt, and pepper. Mix well before serving.

-Nutritional Values: 310 calories | 8g protein | 14g fat | 40g carbohydrates

Recipe 9: Oat and Banana Pancakes

-Prep Time: 20 minutes

-Ingredients: 1 cup of oat flakes | 1 ripe banana | 2 eggs | 1/2 cup of almond milk | 1 teaspoon of baking powder | 1/4 teaspoon of cinnamon | Olive oil for cooking | Maple syrup and fresh fruit for garnish

-Servings: Serves 2-3

-Cooking Method: Stovetop

-Procedure:

Blend the oat flakes into flour. Add the banana, eggs, almond milk, baking powder, and cinnamon to the blender and blend until smooth. Heat some olive oil in a non-stick pan. Pour a ladle of batter for each pancake and cook until bubbles form on the surface. Flip and cook on the other side. Serve the pancakes with maple syrup and fresh fruit.

-Nutritional Values: 270 calories | 10g protein | 7g fat | 45g carbohydrates

Chapter 4:

Sustaining Lunches

Recipe 1: Turmeric Chicken Salad

-Preparation time = 20 minutes

-Ingredients = 2 cups shredded cooked chicken breast | 1/2 cup diced celery | 1/4 cup diced red onion | 1/4 cup Greek yogurt | 1 tablespoon turmeric | Salt and pepper to taste

-Servings = Serves 2

-Mode of cooking: Mixing

-Procedure:

In a large bowl, combine the shredded chicken, celery, red onion, Greek yogurt, and turmeric. Season with salt and pepper to taste. Mix thoroughly until all ingredients are well incorporated. Chill for about 10 minutes before serving to let the flavors meld.

-Nutritional values: 250 calories | 38g protein | 3g fat | 10g carbohydrates

Recipe 2: Quinoa and Black Bean Salad

-Preparation time = 30 minutes

-Ingredients = 1 cup cooked quinoa | 1 cup black beans, rinsed and drained | 1/2 cup cherry tomatoes, halved | 1/4 cup chopped cilantro | 2 tablespoons olive oil | 1 tablespoon lime juice | Salt and pepper to taste

-Servings = Serves 3

-Mode of cooking: Mixing

-Procedure:

In a large bowl, combine cooked quinoa, black beans, cherry tomatoes, and cilantro. In a small bowl, whisk together olive oil, lime juice, salt, and pepper. Pour the dressing over the quinoa mixture and toss to coat evenly. Serve immediately or chill to enhance the flavors.

-Nutritional values: 320 calories | 14g protein | 12g fat | 42g carbohydrates

Recipe 3: Ginger-Soy Salmon Fillets

-Preparation time = 25 minutes

-Ingredients = 2 salmon fillets | 1 tablespoon grated ginger | 2 tablespoons soy sauce (low sodium) | 1 tablespoon honey | 1 clove of garlic, minced | 1 teaspoon olive oil

-Servings = Serves 2

-Mode of cooking: Baking

-Procedure:

Preheat the oven to 375°F (190°C). In a small bowl, mix together ginger, soy sauce, honey, and garlic. Place the salmon fillets in a baking dish and brush them with the olive oil. Pour the ginger-soy mixture over the salmon. Bake for about 15-20 minutes, or until salmon is flaky and cooked through. Serve hot.

-Nutritional values: 300 calories | 25g protein | 15g fat | 10g carbohydrates

Recipe 4: Kale and Avocado Wraps

-Preparation time = 15 minutes

-Ingredients = 4 large kale leaves | 1 ripe avocado, mashed | 1/2 cup sliced cucumber | 1/4 cup shredded carrots | 1 tablespoon lemon juice | Salt and pepper to taste

-Servings = Serves 4

-Mode of cooking: Raw assembly

-Procedure:

Remove the stems from the kale leaves and slightly soften them with your hands. Spread the mashed avocado onto each leaf. Top with cucumber, carrots, and a sprinkle of lemon juice, salt, and pepper. Roll the leaves into wraps, tucking in the edges. Serve immediately for a crunchy and refreshing meal.

-Nutritional values: 150 calories | 4g protein | 11g fat | 12g carbohydrates

Recipe 5: Sweet Potato and Lentil Soup

-Preparation time = 45 minutes

-Ingredients = 1 large sweet potato, peeled and cubed | 1 cup red lentils, rinsed | 1 onion, diced | 2 cloves of garlic, minced | 1 teaspoon cumin | 4 cups vegetable broth | Salt and pepper to taste | 1 tablespoon olive oil

-Servings = Serves 4

-Mode of cooking: Simmering

-Procedure:

Heat the olive oil in a large pot over medium heat. Add onion and garlic, sauté until soft. Add the sweet potato, red lentils, cumin, and vegetable broth. Bring to a boil, then reduce the heat to low and simmer for about 30 minutes, or until sweet potatoes and lentils are tender. Season with salt and pepper. Blend the soup until smooth, using an immersion blender or a standard blender. Serve hot.

- Nutritional values: 280 calories | 14g protein | 3g fat | 50g carbohydrates

Recipe 6: Lemon-Herb Baked Cod

-Preparation time = 30 minutes

-Ingredients = 2 cod fillets | 1 tablespoon olive oil | 1 lemon, juice and zest | 1 teaspoon dried oregano | 1

teaspoon dried thyme | Salt and pepper to taste

-Servings = Serves 2

-Mode of cooking: Baking

-Procedure:
Preheat the oven to 400°F (200°C). Place the cod fillets in a baking dish. In a small bowl, mix olive oil, lemon juice and zest, oregano, thyme, salt, and pepper. Pour the mixture over the cod, ensuring they are well coated. Bake for about 20 minutes or until fish flakes easily with a fork.

-Nutritional values: 200 calories | 22g protein | 10g fat | 2g carbohydrates

Recipe 7: Chopped Veggie Bowl with Hummus

-Preparation time = 15 minutes

-Ingredients = 1 cup mixed greens | 1/2 bell pepper, diced | 1/2 cup cherry tomatoes, halved | 1/4 cup cucumber, diced | 1/4 cup shredded carrots | 2 tablespoons hummus | 1 tablespoon balsamic vinegar | Salt and pepper to taste

-Servings = Serves 1

-Mode of cooking: Raw assembly

-Procedure:
In a large bowl, arrange the mixed greens and top with diced bell pepper, cherry tomatoes, cucumber, and shredded carrots. Dollop the hummus in the center. Drizzle balsamic vinegar over the salad. Season with salt and pepper to taste. Toss to combine when ready to eat.

-Nutritional values: 180 calories | 5g protein | 8g fat | 24g carbohydrates

Recipe 8: Spiced Lentil Stew with Kale

-Preparation time = 35 minutes

- Ingredients = 1 cup green lentils | 1 bunch kale, stems removed and chopped | 1 onion, diced | 2 cloves garlic, minced | 1 teaspoon ground turmeric | 1 teaspoon smoked paprika | 1 tablespoon olive oil | 4 cups vegetable broth | Salt and pepper to taste

-Servings = Serves 4

-Mode of cooking: Simmering

-Procedure:
In a large pot, heat the olive oil over medium heat. Add the onion and garlic,

and cook until soft. Stir in turmeric and paprika. Add the green lentils and vegetable broth. Bring to a boil then reduce heat and simmer for 25 minutes. Add the chopped kale in the last 5 minutes of cooking. Season with salt and pepper. Cook until the lentils are tender and the kale has wilted.

-Nutritional values: 250 calories | 18g protein | 4g fat | 40g carbohydrates

Recipe 9: Mediterranean Chickpea Salad

-Preparation time = 15 minutes

-Ingredients = 1 can chickpeas, rinsed and drained | 1/2 cup diced cucumber | 1/2 cup halved cherry tomatoes | 1/4 cup chopped red onion | 1/4 cup chopped parsley | 3 tablespoons lemon juice | 2 tablespoons extra virgin olive oil | Salt and pepper to taste

-Servings = Serves 3

-Mode of cooking: Mixing

-Procedure:

In a large bowl, mix the chickpeas, cucumber, cherry tomatoes, red onion, and parsley. In a small bowl, whisk together the lemon juice, olive oil, salt, and pepper to make the dressing. Pour the dressing over the salad and toss until everything is evenly coated. Serve chilled or at room temperature.

-Nutritional values: 220 calories | 8g protein | 9g fat | 29g carbohydrates

Recipe 10: Roasted Vegetable Quinoa Bowl

-Preparation time = 40 minutes

-Ingredients = 1/2 cup quinoa (uncooked) | 1/2 cup diced sweet potatoes | 1/2 cup cauliflower florets | 1/2 red bell pepper, sliced | 1 tablespoon avocado oil | 1 teaspoon garlic powder |

Salt and pepper to taste | 1 tablespoon tahini for dressing

-Servings = Serves 2

-Mode of cooking: Roasting & Boiling

-Procedure:
Preheat the oven to 400°F (200°C). Toss the sweet potatoes, cauliflower, and red bell pepper with avocado oil, garlic powder, salt, and pepper. Spread the vegetables on a baking sheet and roast for about 25 minutes, or until tender and lightly browned. Meanwhile, cook the quinoa according to package instructions. Combine the roasted vegetables with the cooked quinoa. Drizzle tahini over the top before serving.

-Nutritional values: 330 calories | 10g protein | 14g fat | 45g carbohydrates

Chapter 5:

Balanced Dinners

Recipe 1: Grilled Salmon with Asparagus

-Preparation time = 20 minutes

-Ingredients = 2 salmon fillets | 1 bunch asparagus | 1 tablespoon olive oil | Lemon slices | Salt and pepper

-Servings = Serves 2

Mode of cooking: Grilling

-Procedure:
Preheat grill. Brush salmon and asparagus with olive oil, season with salt and pepper, and place on the grill. Cook salmon for about 6-8 minutes on each side and asparagus for about 5 minutes, turning once. Serve with lemon slices.

-Nutritional values: 350 calories | 34g protein | 22g fat| 4g carbohydrates

Recipe 2: Chicken and Quinoa Salad

-Preparation time = 30 minutes

-Ingredients = 2 cups cooked quinoa | 2 chicken breasts, grilled and sliced | 1 cup cherry tomatoes | 1 avocado, diced | 1/4 cup chopped basil | 2 tablespoons balsamic vinegar | 1 tablespoon olive oil | Salt and pepper

-Servings = Serves 2

-Mode of cooking: Mixing

-Procedure:

In a large bowl, combine quinoa, sliced chicken, cherry tomatoes, avocado, and basil. Dress with balsamic vinegar and olive oil, toss to combine. Season with salt and pepper to taste.

-Nutritional values: 400 calories | 35g protein | 20g fat| 30g carbohydrates

Recipe 3: Turmeric Cauliflower Steak

-Preparation time = 35 minutes

-Ingredients = 2 large cauliflower slices | 1 teaspoon turmeric | 1/2 teaspoon garlic powder | 2 tablespoons olive oil | Salt and pepper

-Servings = Serves 2

-Mode of cooking: Baking

-Procedure:

Preheat oven to 400°F (200°C). Mix olive oil, turmeric, garlic powder, salt, and pepper. Brush mixture on both sides of the cauliflower steaks. Bake for 30 minutes or until tender and golden.

-Nutritional values: 210 calories | 5g protein | 14g fat| 18g carbohydrates

Recipe 4: Spinach and Salmon Stir-Fry

-Preparation time = 25 minutes

-Ingredients = 2 salmon fillets, cubed | 3 cups spinach | 1 tablespoon olive oil | 2 cloves garlic, minced | 1 tablespoon soy sauce | 1 tablespoon sesame seeds | Salt and pepper

-Servings = Serves 2

-Mode of cooking: Stir-frying

-Procedure:

Heat olive oil in a pan over medium heat. Add garlic and salmon, cook until salmon is nearly done. Add spinach, soy sauce, and season with salt and pepper. Cook until spinach wilts. Sprinkle with sesame seeds before serving.

-Nutritional values: 295 calories | 27g protein | 17g fat| 4g carbohydrates

Recipe 5: Zucchini Noodles with Pesto

-Preparation time = 15 minutes

-Ingredients = 4 zucchinis, spiraled into noodles | 1/2 cup basil pesto | 1/4 cup pine nuts | Salt and pepper

-Servings = Serves 4

-Mode of cooking: Sautéing

-Procedure:
Heat zucchini noodles in a pan over medium heat for about 5-7 minutes. Remove from heat and mix with basil pesto. Season with salt and pepper and garnish with pine nuts.

-Nutritional values: 180 calories | 4g protcin | 14g fat| 10g carbohydrates

Recipe 6: Beetroot and Feta Salad

-Preparation time = 15 minutes

-Ingredients = 3 beets, cooked and sliced | 1 cup arugula | 1/2 cup feta cheese, crumbled | 2 tablespoons walnut oil | 1 tablespoon lemon juice | Salt and pepper

-Servings = Serves 2

-Mode of cooking: Mixing

-Procedure:
Combine beets, arugula, and feta cheese in a salad bowl. Dress with walnut oil and lemon juice, toss gently. Season with salt and pepper to taste.

-Nutritional values: 210 calories | 7g protein | 15g fat| 12g carbohydrates

Recipe 7: Ginger Tofu Stir-Fry

-Preparation time = 20 minutes

-Ingredients = 400g tofu, diced | 2 cups broccoli, florets | 1 red bell pepper, sliced | 2 tablespoons olive oil | 1 tablespoon grated ginger | 2 tablespoons soy sauce | Salt and pepper

-Servings = Serves 2

-Mode of cooking: Stir-frying

-Procedure:
Heat olive oil in a pan over medium heat. Add grated ginger and tofu, fry

until golden. Add broccoli and bell pepper, cook for about 7 minutes. Drizzle with soy sauce, season with salt and pepper, and stir until vegetables are tender.

Nutritional values: 280 calories | 19g protein | 20g fat| 12g carbohydrates

Recipe 8: Lemon Herb Grilled Chicken

-Preparation time = 45 minutes (includes marinating time)

-Ingredients = 2 chicken breasts | Juice of 1 lemon | 2 tablespoons olive oil | 1 teaspoon dried herbs (such as thyme and basil) | Salt and pepper

-Servings = Serves 2

-Mode of cooking: Grilling

-Procedure:
Marinate chicken breasts with lemon juice, olive oil, dried herbs, salt, and

pepper for at least 30 minutes. Grill over medium heat for about 6-7 minutes on each side or until fully cooked.

-Nutritional values: 240 calories | 26g protein | 14g fat| 2g carbohydrates

Recipe 9: Roasted Pepper and Hummus Wrap

-Preparation time = 15 minutes

-Ingredients = 2 whole grain wraps | 1 cup hummus | 1 red bell pepper, roasted and sliced | 1 yellow bell pepper, roasted and sliced | 1 handful spinach | Salt and pepper

-Servings = Serves 2

-Mode of cooking: Assembling

-Procedure:
Spread hummus on wraps. Lay roasted peppers and spinach down the center. Season with salt and pepper. Wrap tightly and slice in half.

-Nutritional values: 320 calories | 10g protein | 15g fat| 35g carbohydrates

Recipe 10: Coconut Curry Vegetable Stew

-Preparation time = 40 minutes

-Ingredients = 1 tablespoon coconut oil | 1 onion, chopped | 2 cloves garlic, minced | 1 tablespoon curry powder | 1 can coconut milk | 2 cups vegetable broth | 1 cup cauliflower florets | 1 cup diced carrots | 1 cup green beans | Salt and pepper

-Servings = Serves 4

-Mode of cooking: Simmering

-Procedure:

In a large pot, heat coconut oil over medium heat. Add onion and garlic, cook until soft. Stir in curry powder, then add coconut milk and vegetable broth. Bring to a boil, add vegetables, and simmer for 25 minutes. Season with salt and pepper.

-Nutritional values: 250 calories | 4g protein | 21g fat| 18g carbohydrates

Chapter 6 :

Snacks

Recipe 1: Almond Butter and Banana Slices

-**Preparation time** = 5 minutes

-**Ingredients** = 1 banana | 2 tablespoons almond butter

-**Servings** = Serves 1

-**Mode of cooking:** Assembly

-**Procedure:** Slice the banana. Spread almond butter over each slice. Enjoy as a quick and healthy snack.

-**Nutritional values:** 280 calories | 8g protein | 18g fats | 24g carbohydrates

Recipe 2: Avocado and Tomato Toast

-**Preparation time** = 10 minutes

-**Ingredients** = 1 slice whole grain bread | 1/2 ripe avocado | 1 tomato

-**Servings** = Serves 1

-**Mode of cooking:** Toasting

-**Procedure:** Toast the bread. Mash the avocado and spread it over the toast. Top with sliced tomato. Season with salt and pepper if desired.

-**Nutritional values:** 220 calories | 6g protein | 12g fats | 26g carbohydrates

Recipe 3: Greek Yogurt with Walnuts and Honey

-**Preparation time** = 5 minutes

-**Ingredients** = 1 cup Greek yogurt (plain) | 1/4 cup walnuts | 1 tablespoon honey

-**Servings** = Serves 1

-**Mode of cooking:** Mixing

-**Procedure:** Mix Greek yogurt with walnuts. Drizzle honey on top for sweetness.

-**Nutritional values:** 310 calories | 20g protein | 18g fats | 22g carbohydrates

Recipe 4: Cucumber and Hummus Cups

-**Preparation time** = 10 minutes

-**Ingredients** = 1 large cucumber | 1/2 cup hummus

-**Servings** = Serves 2

-**Mode of cooking:** Assembly

-**Procedure:** Slice cucumber into thick rounds. Scoop a small amount from the center of each slice and fill with hummus.

-**Nutritional values:** 150 calories | 6g protein | 9g fats | 12g carbohydrates

Recipe 5: Berries and Almond Mix

-**Preparation time** = 5 minutes

-**Ingredients** = 1/2 cup mixed berries | 1/4 cup almonds

-**Servings** = Serves 1

-**Mode of cooking:** Mixing

-**Procedure:** Simply mix fresh or frozen berries with almonds for a quick snack.

-**Nutritional values:** 200 calories | 6g protein | 12g fats | 18g carbohydrates

Recipe 6: Spinach and Feta Stuffed Mushrooms

-**Preparation time** = 20 minutes

-**Ingredients** = 6 large mushrooms | 1/2 cup spinach | 1/4 cup crumbled feta cheese | 1 tablespoon olive oil

-**Servings** = Serves 2

-**Mode of cooking:** Baking

-**Procedure:** Preheat oven to 350°F (175°C). Remove stems from mushrooms. Mix spinach and feta, stuff into mushrooms, drizzle with olive oil. Bake for 15 minutes.

-**Nutritional values:** 160 calories | 8g protein | 12g fats | 4g carbohydrates

Recipe 7: Turmeric and Honey Roasted Nuts

-Preparation time = 30 minutes

-Ingredients = 1/2 cup mixed nuts | 1 teaspoon turmeric | 2 tablespoons honey

-Servings = Serves 2

-Mode of cooking: Roasting

-Procedure: Preheat oven to 300°F (150°C). Mix nuts with turmeric and honey. Spread on a baking sheet and roast for 20 minutes, stirring halfway.

-Nutritional values: 310 calories | 8g protein | 22g fats | 24g carbohydrates

Recipe 8: Chia Seed Pudding

-Preparation time = 15 minutes (plus overnight soaking)

-Ingredients = 1/4 cup chia seeds | 1 cup almond milk | 1 tablespoon maple syrup

-Servings = Serves 2

-Mode of cooking: Soaking

-Procedure: Mix chia seeds, almond milk, and maple syrup in a bowl. Refrigerate overnight. Stir before serving.

-Nutritional values: 240 calories | 6g protein | 14g fats | 24g carbohydrates

Recipe 9: Smoked Salmon and Cucumber Rolls

-Preparation time = 15 minutes

-Ingredients = 4 slices smoked salmon | 1 cucumber | 1 tablespoon cream cheese (dairy-free if desired)

-Servings = Serves 2

-Mode of cooking: Rolling

-Procedure: Slice cucumber into long, thin strips using a vegetable peeler. Spread a thin layer of cream cheese on each salmon slice, place a strip of cucumber on top, and roll up.

-Nutritional values: 150 calories | 12g protein | 8g fats | 4g carbohydrates

Recipe 10: Kale Chips

-Preparation time = 30 minutes

-Ingredients = 1 bunch kale | 1 tablespoon olive oil | Salt (to taste)

-Servings = Serves 2

-Mode of cooking: Baking

-Procedure: Preheat oven to 300°F (150°C). Tear kale into bite-size pieces, toss with olive oil and salt. Spread on a baking sheet and bake for 20-25 minutes, until crisp.

-Nutritional values: 110 calories | 4g protein | 7g fats | 10g carbohydrates

Chapter 7 :

Thirst-Quenching Drinks and Beneficial Herbal Teas

Recipe 1: Ginger Turmeric Tea.

-Preparation time = 10 minutes

-Ingredients = 1 teaspoon grated ginger | 1 teaspoon turmeric | 1 cup water | Honey (optional)

-Servings = Serves 1

-Mode of cooking: Simmering

-Procedure: Boil water and add grated ginger and turmeric. Simmer for 5 minutes, then strain into a cup. Add honey to taste if desired.

-Nutritional values: < 50 calories | < 1g protein | < 1g fats | < 1g carbohydrates

Recipe 2: Anti-Inflammatory Berry Smoothie.

-Preparation time = 5 minutes

-Ingredients = 1/2 cup mixed berries | 1 cup spinach | 1 cup almond milk | 1 tablespoon chia seeds

-Servings = Serves 1

-Mode of cooking: Blending

-Procedure: Combine all ingredients in a blender and blend until smooth.

-Nutritional values: 150 calories | 3g protein | 4g fats | 27g carbohydrates

Recipe 3: Green Tea and Lemon Infusion.

-Preparation time = 5 minutes

-Ingredients = 1 green tea bag | 1/2 lemon | 1 cup boiling water

-Servings = Serves 1

-Mode of cooking: Steeping

-Procedure: Steep the green tea bag and half a lemon's juice in boiling water for 3 minutes. Remove the tea bag and enjoy.

-Nutritional values: < 10 calories | < 1g protein | < 1g fats | 3g carbohydrates

Recipe 4: Cucumber Mint Water.

-Preparation time = 5 minutes (plus chilling)

-Ingredients = 1/2 cucumber | 10 mint leaves | 1 liter water

-Servings = Serves 4

-Mode of cooking: Infusion

-Procedure: Slice cucumber and add to a pitcher with mint leaves and water. Chill for an hour before serving.

-Nutritional values: < 10 calories | < 1g protein | < 1g fats | < 1g carbohydrates

Recipe 5: Chamomile Lavender Tea.

-Preparation time = 10 minutes

-Ingredients = 1 teaspoon chamomile flowers | 1/2 teaspoon lavender buds | 1 cup water

-Servings = Serves 1

-Mode of cooking: Steeping

-Procedure: Bring water to a boil, add chamomile and lavender, and let steep for 5 minutes. Strain and serve.

-Nutritional values: < 5 calories | < 1g protein | < 1g fats | < 1g carbohydrates

Recipe 6: Lemon Ginger Detox Drink.

-Preparation time = 5 minutes

-Ingredients = 1 lemon | 1 teaspoon grated ginger | 1 cup hot water | 1 teaspoon honey (optional)

-Servings = Serves 1

-Mode of cooking: Mixing

-Procedure: Combine the juice of the lemon with grated ginger in a mug. Pour hot water over it, stir, and add honey if desired.

-Nutritional values: 25 calories | < 1g protein | < 1g fats | 6g carbohydrates

Recipe 7: Hibiscus and Rosehip Tea.

-Preparation time = 10 minutes

-Ingredients = 1 teaspoon hibiscus flowers | 1 teaspoon rosehip | 1 cup water

-Servings = Serves 1

-Mode of cooking: Steeping

-Procedure: Boil water and pour over hibiscus and rosehip in a cup. Steep for 5 minutes, strain, and serve.

-Nutritional values: < 5 calories | < 1g protein | < 1g fats | 1g carbohydrates

Recipe 8: Matcha Mint Tea.

-Preparation time = 5 minutes

-Ingredients = 1 teaspoon matcha powder | 5 mint leaves | 1 cup hot water

-Servings = Serves 1

-Mode of cooking: Whisking

-Procedure: Whisk matcha powder with a little cold water until a paste forms. Add hot water and mint leaves, then whisk briskly until frothy.

-Nutritional values: 30 calories | 3g protein | < 1g fats | 4g carbohydrates

Recipe 9: Iced Ginger Peach Tea.

-Preparation time = 10 minutes (plus cooling)

-Ingredients = 1 black tea bag | 1 ripe peach | 1/2 teaspoon grated ginger | 1 cup water | Ice cubes

-Servings = Serves 1

-Mode of cooking: Infusing

-Procedure: Steep the tea bag, ginger, and half a sliced peach in boiling water for 5 minutes. Remove the tea bag and let cool. Pour over ice and garnish with the remaining peach slices.

-Nutritional values: 40 calories | < 1g protein | < 1g fats | 10g carbohydrates

Recipe 10: Cooling Cilantro Lime Drink.

-Preparation time = 5 minutes

-Ingredients = 1/2 cup cilantro leaves | Juice of 2 limes | 1 teaspoon honey | 1 cup cold water | Ice cubes

-Servings = Serves 1

-Mode of cooking: Blending

-Procedure: Blend cilantro, lime juice, honey, and water until smooth. Strain over a glass with ice cubes and serve.

-Nutritional values: 25 calories | < 1g protein | < 1g fats | 6g carbohydrates

Chapter 8 :

Quick Meals for Those Short on Time

Recipe 1: Quinoa and Black Bean Salad.

-**Preparation time**: 15 minutes

-**Ingredients**: 1 cup cooked quinoa, 1/2 cup black beans, 1/2 cup diced tomatoes, 1/4 cup chopped red onion, 1 tablespoon olive oil, Juice of 1 lime, Salt and pepper to taste

-**Servings**: Serves 2

-**Mode of cooking**: Mixing

-**Procedure**: In a large bowl, combine all ingredients and mix well. Season with salt and pepper to taste.

-**Nutritional values**: 220 calories, 8g protein, 7g fat, 33g carbohydrates

Recipe 2: Spinach and Avocado Smoothie.

-**Preparation time**: 5 minutes

-**Ingredients**: 1 cup spinach, 1/2 avocado, 1/2 banana, 1 cup almond milk, 1 tablespoon chia seeds

-**Servings**: Serves 1

-**Mode of cooking**: Blending

-**Procedure**: Combine all ingredients in a blender and blend until smooth.

-**Nutritional values**: 240 calories, 5g protein, 14g fat, 27g carbohydrates

Recipe 3: Mediterranean Chickpea Wrap.

-**Preparation time**: 10 minutes

-Ingredients: 1 whole grain wrap, 1/2 cup chickpeas, 1/4 cup diced cucumber, 1/4 cup diced tomato, 1 tablespoon tahini, Lemon juice to taste, Salt and pepper to taste

-Servings: Serves 1

-Mode of cooking: Wrapping

-Procedure: Spread tahini on the wrap, top with chickpeas, cucumber, and tomato. Drizzle with lemon juice, season with salt and pepper, and roll up.

-Nutritional values: 320 calories, 12g protein, 14g fat, 42g carbohydrates

Recipe 4: Garlic Lemon Salmon.

-Preparation time: 15 minutes

-Ingredients: 1 salmon fillet, 1 tablespoon olive oil, 1 clove garlic, minced, Juice of 1/2 lemon, Salt and pepper to taste

-Servings: Serves 1

-Mode of cooking: Baking

-Procedure: Preheat oven to 392°F (200°C). Place salmon on a baking sheet. Mix olive oil, garlic, and lemon juice, then pour over salmon. Season with salt and pepper. Bake for 12 minutes.

-Nutritional values: 280 calories, 23g protein, 20g fat, 0g carbohydrates

Recipe 5: Tofu Stir-Fry with Vegetables.

-Preparation time: 15 minutes

-Ingredients: 1/2 block firm tofu, cubed, 1 cup mixed vegetables (bell pepper, broccoli, carrot), 1 tablespoon olive oil, 2 tablespoons soy sauce (gluten-free)

-Servings: Serves 1

-Mode of cooking: Stir-frying

-Procedure: Heat oil in a pan, add tofu, and cook until golden. Add vegetables and stir-fry until tender. Stir in soy sauce and serve.

-Nutritional values: 250 calories, 18g protein, 15g fat, 10g carbohydrates

Recipe 6: Avocado Toast with Poached Egg.

-Preparation time: 10 minutes

-Ingredients: 1 slice whole grain bread, 1/2 avocado, mashed, 1 egg, 1 teaspoon vinegar, Salt and pepper to taste

-Servings: Serves 1

-Mode of cooking: Poaching, Toasting

-Procedure: Toast bread, spread mashed avocado. Poach egg in boiling water with vinegar for 3 minutes. Place on toast, season with salt and pepper.

-Nutritional values: 300 calories, 13g protein, 20g fat, 23g carbohydrates

Recipe 7: Sweet Potato and Black Bean Burrito.

-Preparation time: 15 minutes

-Ingredients: 1 small sweet potato, cubed, 1/2 cup black beans, 1 whole grain tortilla, 1/4 cup diced red pepper, 1/4 teaspoon cumin, Salt to taste

-Servings: Serves 1

-Mode of cooking: Microwaving, Wrapping

-Procedure: Microwave sweet potato until tender, about 5 minutes. Mix with black beans, red pepper, and cumin. Season with salt, wrap in tortilla.

-Nutritional values: 290 calories, 10g protein, 3g fat, 54g carbohydrates

Recipe 8: Cucumber and Hummus Sandwich.

-Preparation time: 5 minutes

-Ingredients: 2 slices whole grain bread, 1/4 cup hummus, 1/2 cucumber, sliced, Salt and pepper to taste

-Servings: Serves 1

-Mode of cooking: Assembling

-Procedure: Spread hummus on both bread slices, layer cucumber slices, season with salt and pepper. Assemble sandwich.

-Nutritional values: 250 calories, 10g protein, 6g fat, 40g carbohydrates

Recipe 9: Broccoli and Almond Salad.

-Preparation time: 10 minutes

-Ingredients: 1 cup chopped broccoli, 1/4 cup sliced almonds, 1 tablespoon olive oil, 1 tablespoon lemon juice, Salt and pepper to taste

-Servings: Serves 1

-Mode of cooking: Mixing

-Procedure: Combine broccoli, almonds, olive oil, and lemon juice in a bowl. Season with salt and pepper and mix well.

-Nutritional values: 230 calories, 6g protein, 20g fat, 8g carbohydrates

-Preparation time: 15 minutes

-Ingredients: 1 cup spiralized zucchini (zoodles), 100g shrimp, peeled, 1 tablespoon olive oil, 1/2 teaspoon red pepper flakes, Salt and pepper to taste

-Servings: Serves 1

-Mode of cooking: Sautéing

-Procedure: Heat oil in a pan, add shrimp and red pepper flakes, cook until shrimp is pink. Add zoodles, sauté for 2-3 minutes. Season with salt and pepper.

-Nutritional values: 220 calories, 24g protein, 12g fat, 5g carbohydrates

Recipe 10: Spicy Shrimp Zoodles.

Chapter 9 :

Vegetarian and Vegan Options

Recipe 1: Turmeric Quinoa with Roasted Vegetables

-Preparation time = 25 minutes

-Ingredients = 1 cup quinoa | 1/2 teaspoon turmeric | 2 cups mixed vegetables (zucchini, bell pepper, broccoli) | 1 tablespoon olive oil | Salt and pepper

-Servings = Serves 2

-Mode of cooking: Baking and Boiling

-Procedure: Preheat the oven to 200°C. Toss the mixed vegetables with olive oil, salt, and pepper, then roast for 20 minutes. Cook quinoa with turmeric and salt. Mix roasted vegetables with cooked quinoa.

-Nutritional values: 310 calories | 10g protein | 8g fat | 48g carbohydrates

Recipe 2: Avocado and Kale Salad

-Preparation time = 15 minutes

-Ingredients = 2 cups kale | 1 ripe avocado | 1 tablespoon lemon juice | 1/4 cup sliced almonds | Salt and pepper

-Servings = Serves 1

-Mode of cooking: Tossing

-Procedure: Massage kale with lemon juice and a pinch of salt. Add avocado slices and almonds. Season with salt and pepper, then toss gently.

-Nutritional values: 280 calories | 6g protein | 24g fat | 18g carbohydrates

Recipe 3: Chickpea and Sweet Potato Curry

-Preparation time = 30 minutes

-Ingredients = 1/2 sweet potato | 1 cup chickpeas (cooked) | 1 tablespoon curry powder | 1 can coconut milk | 1/2 red onion

-Servings = Serves 2

-Mode of cooking: Boiling

-Procedure: Sauté onion until translucent. Add diced sweet potato, chickpeas, curry powder, and coconut milk. Simmer until sweet potato is tender.

-Nutritional values: 360 calories | 9g protein | 18g fat | 42g carbohydrates

Recipe 4: Lentil and Spinach Soup

-Preparation time = 40 minutes

-Ingredients = 1 cup lentils | 2 cups vegetable broth | 1 cup spinach leaves | 1/2 teaspoon cumin | 1 garlic clove

-Servings = Serves 2

-Mode of cooking: Boiling

-Procedure: Cook lentils in vegetable broth with cumin and minced garlic until tender. Add spinach and simmer until wilted.

-Nutritional values: 230 calories | 14g protein | 1g fat | 40g carbohydrates

Recipe 5: Zucchini Noodles with Pesto

-Preparation time = 15 minutes

-Ingredients = 2 zucchinis (spiraled) | 1/4 cup pesto (vegan) | 1/4 cup cherry tomatoes | 1 table spoon pine nuts | Salt and pepper

-Servings = Serves 2

-Mode of cooking: Tossing

-Procedure: Toss zucchini noodles with vegan pesto. Add halved cherry tomatoes and pine nuts. Season with salt and pepper.

-Nutritional values: 150 calories | 4g protein | 12g fat | 8g carbohydrates

Recipe 6: Butternut Squash and Black Bean Enchiladas

-Preparation time = 45 minutes

-Ingredients = 1 cup cubed butternut squash | 1/2 cup black beans | 2 whole grain tortillas | 1/2 cup enchilada sauce | 1/4 cup cashew cheese

-Servings = Serves 2

-Mode of cooking: Baking

-Procedure: Fill tortillas with butternut squash and black beans. Top with enchilada sauce and cashew cheese. Bake at 200°C for 20 minutes.

-Nutritional values: 320 calories | 9g protein | 9g fat | 52g carbohydrates

Recipe 7: Cauliflower Steak with Herb Salsa

-**Preparation time** = 25 minutes

-**Ingredients** = 2 cauliflower steaks | 1 tablespoon olive oil | 1/4 cup herb salsa (parsley, cilantro, garlic, lemon juice) | Salt and pepper

-**Servings** = Serves 2

-Mode of cooking: Grilling

-**Procedure**: Grill cauliflower steaks with olive oil until tender. Serve with herb salsa on top.

-**Nutritional values**: 150 calories | 5g protein | 7g fat | 18g carbohydrates

Recipe 8: Vegan Mushroom Stroganoff

-**Preparation time** = 30 minutes

-**Ingredients** = 2 cups sliced mushrooms | 1 cup onion, chopped | 1 garlic clove | 1 cup vegetable broth | 1/2 cup coconut cream | 1 tablespoon tamari sauce

-**Servings** = Serves 2

-**Mode of cooking**: Sautéing

-**Procedure**: Sauté onion, garlic, and mushrooms. Add vegetable broth and

simmer. Stir in coconut cream and tamari, cook until thickened.

-**Nutritional values**: 220 calories | 5g protein | 14g fat | 20g carbohydrates

Recipe 9: Beets and Quinoa Salad

-**Preparation time** = 20 minutes

-Ingredients = 1 cup cooked quinoa | 1/2 cup roasted beets, cubed | 1/4 cup walnut pieces | 1 tablespoon balsamic vinegar | 1 tablespoon olive oil

-**Servings** = Serves 2

-**Mode of cooking**: Tossing

-**Procedure**: Combine quinoa, beets, and walnuts. Dress with balsamic vinegar and olive oil.

-**Nutritional values**: 310 calories | 8g protein | 18g fat | 32g carbohydrates

Recipe 10: Spiced Apple Overnight Oats

-**Preparation time** = 10 minutes (+overnight soaking)

-**Ingredients** = 1 cup rolled oats | 1 cup almond milk | 1 apple, grated | 1/2 teaspoon cinnamon | 1 tablespoon chia seeds

-Servings = Serves 2

-Mode of cooking: Soaking

-Procedure: Mix all ingredients in a jar. Refrigerate overnight. Stir before serving.

-Nutritional values: 250 calories | 6g protein | 5g fat | 45g carbohydrates

Chapter 10

Special Recipes for Holidays and Occasions

Recipe 1: Festive Quinoa Stuffed Peppers

-Preparation time = 45 minutes

-Ingredients = 4 large bell peppers | 1 cup quinoa | 1/2 cup black beans | 1/2 cup corn | 1 teaspoon cumin | 1/2 teaspoon chili flakes | 1/4 cup fresh cilantro

-Servings = Serves 4

-Mode of cooking: Baking and Boiling

-Procedure: Cook quinoa and mix with black beans, corn, cumin, chili flakes, and cilantro. Halve bell peppers and stuff with the mixture. Bake at 180°C for 25 minutes.

-Nutritional values: 220 calories | 8g protein | 2g fat | 42g carbohydrates

Recipe 2: Anti-inflammatory Holiday Nut Roast

-Preparation time = 60 minutes

-Ingredients = 1 cup mixed nuts (walnuts, almonds) | 1 cup lentils | 1/2 cup breadcrumbs | 2 tablespoons olive oil | 1 teaspoon turmeric | 2 cloves garlic | 1/2 teaspoon sage

-Servings = Serves 6

-Mode of cooking: Baking

-Procedure: Process nuts until coarse, mix with cooked lentils, breadcrumbs, olive oil, turmeric, minced garlic, and sage. Press into loaf pan, bake at 180°C for 40 minutes.

-Nutritional values: 280 calories | 9g protein | 18g fat | 24g carbohydrates

Recipe 3: Golden Turmeric Latkes

-Preparation time = 30 minutes

-Ingredients = 2 large potatoes | 1 teaspoon turmeric | 1/4 cup onion, grated | 2 tablespoons olive oil | Salt and pepper

-**Servings** = Serves 4

-**Mode of cooking**: Pan-frying

-**Procedure**: Grate potatoes, mix with turmeric, onion, salt, and pepper. Form into patties and fry in olive oil until golden.

-**Nutritional values**: 150 calories | 2g protein | 7g fat | 20g carbohydrates

Recipe 4: Gingerbread Quinoa Porridge

-**Preparation time** = 20 minutes

-**Ingredients** = 1 cup quinoa | 1 teaspoon ginger | 1/2 teaspoon cinnamon | 2 tablespoons maple syrup | 1 cup almond milk

-**Servings** = Serves 4

-**Mode of cooking**: Boiling

- Procedure: Cook quinoa in almond milk with ginger and cinnamon. Sweeten with maple syrup. Serve warm.

-**Nutritional values**: 210 calories | 6g protein | 3g fat | 40g carbohydrates

Recipe 5: Winter Berry Salad with Walnut Dressing

-**Preparation time** = 15 minutes

-**Ingredients** = 2 cups mixed greens (spinach, kale) | 1/2 cup mixed berries (strawberries, blueberries) | 1/4 cup walnuts | 2 tablespoons balsamic

vinegar | 1 tablespoon olive oil | 1 teaspoon honey

-**Servings** = Serves 4

-**Mode of cooking**: Tossing

-**Procedure**: Toss greens and berries. Blend walnuts, balsamic vinegar, olive oil, and honey for dressing. Drizzle over salad.

-**Nutritional values**: 180 calories | 4g protein | 12g fat | 18g carbohydrates

Recipe 6: Roasted Brussels Sprouts with Pomegranate

-**Preparation time** = 40 minutes

-**Ingredients** = 2 cups Brussels sprouts | 1 tablespoon olive oil | Salt and pepper | 1/2 cup pomegranate seeds | 1 teaspoon balsamic glaze

-**Servings** = Serves 4

-**Mode of cooking**: Roasting

-**Procedure**: Toss Brussels sprouts with olive oil, salt, and pepper. Roast at 200°C for 35 minutes. Top with pomegranate seeds and balsamic glaze.

-**Nutritional values**: 110 calories | 3g protein | 5g fat | 15g carbohydrates

Recipe 7: Cinnamon Apple Slices with Almond Butter

-Preparation time = 10 minutes

-Ingredients = 2 apples | 1/2 teaspoon cinnamon | 2 tablespoons almond butter

-Servings = Serves 4

-Mode of cooking: Raw

-Procedure: Slice apples, sprinkle with cinnamon. Serve with almond butter for dipping.

-Nutritional values: 150 calories | 2g protein | 8g fat | 20g carbohydrates

Recipe 8: Savory Pumpkin Soup

-Preparation time = 50 minutes

-Ingredients = 2 cups pumpkin puree | 1 cup vegetable broth | 1/2 cup coconut milk | 1 teaspoon ginger | Salt and pepper

-Servings = Serves 4

-Mode of cooking: Boiling

-Procedure: Combine pumpkin, broth, coconut milk, and ginger in a pot. Bring to boil, simmer for 45 minutes. Season with salt and pepper.

-Nutritional values: 120 calories | 2g protein | 7g fat | 15g carbohydrates

Recipe 9: Stuffed Sweet Potatoes with Greens and Beans

-Preparation time = 1 hour

-Ingredients = 4 sweet potatoes | 1 cup kale, chopped | 1/2 cup black beans | 1/2 teaspoon paprika | 1 tablespoon olive oil | Salt and pepper

-Servings = Serves 4

-Mode of cooking: Baking

-Procedure: Bake sweet potatoes at 200°C for 45 minutes. Sauté kale and black beans in olive oil, season with paprika, salt, and pepper. Stuff into baked sweet potatoes.

-Nutritional values: 250 calories | 5g protein | 4g fat | 48g carbohydrates

Recipe 10: Festive Cranberry and Almond Bark

-Preparation time = 20 minutes (+ freezing time)

-Ingredients = 1 cup dark chocolate (min 70% cocoa) | 1/2 cup dried cranberries | 1/4 cup sliced almonds

-Servings = Serves 8

-Mode of cooking: Freezing

-Procedure: Melt dark chocolate, spread onto baking sheet. Sprinkle with cranberries and almonds. Freeze until set.

-Nutritional values: 150 calories | 2g protein | 9g fat | 17g carbohydrates

Chapter 11

Preparing for the Detox Plan

11.1 What to Expect During Detox

What to Expect During Detox

Embarking on a detox plan is not just a step towards better health—it's a commitment to resetting your body and giving it a fresh start. However, before you plunge into this transformative journey, it's crucial to set realistic expectations and understand what lies ahead. This chapter aims to hold your hand through the detox terrain, guiding you, a person over 50, through the anticipated experiences, both challenging and rewarding, ensuring you're well-prepared and confident to move forward.

The Initial Adjustment Phase

Detoxification, especially for those over 50, can be likened to spring cleaning your house after a long winter. Just as you might encounter dust and clutter that's been building up over months, your body will begin to purge toxins that have been accumulating over years. During the first few days, it's common to experience withdrawal symptoms from caffeine, sugar, and processed foods. These might manifest as headaches, fatigue, irritability, or cravings. It's your body's natural reaction to suddenly being denied what it's been accustomed to.

Understanding this phase is crucial. Instead of viewing these symptoms as negative side effects, interpret them as signs that your body is diligently working to eliminate toxins and repair itself. Hydration is key here—drinking plenty of water will help flush out impurities and ease the transition.

The Emotional Roller Coaster

Detox isn't just about the physical. It's a holistic journey that encompasses emotional well-being. The process can stir up unexpected emotional responses. You might find yourself feeling more sensitive than usual or revisiting emotions you thought you had long buried. This is normal. The foods we eat can significantly affect our mood and emotions, and as you change your diet, your emotional landscape might shift as well. Embrace this as part of the healing process. It's an opportunity to confront and release emotions that you may have been suppressing with food.

The Physical Transformation

As your body adapts to the detox, you'll begin to notice remarkable changes. Energy levels may start to rise as your system isn't bogged down by the task of processing heavy, unhealthy foods. You might experience improved sleep quality, since a cleaner diet promotes better sleep cycles. Additionally, don't be surprised if you start to see visible changes. Clearer skin, weight loss, and a more vibrant complexion are frequently reported benefits of a successful detox plan.

One fascinating aspect for individuals over 50 is the potential improvement in pain and inflammation. Many find that aches and pains they've attributed to aging significantly lessen or disappear altogether. This is a testament to the power of food as medicine—by eliminating inflammatory foods and incorporating nutrient-dense options, you're allowing your body to heal and reduce inflammation naturally.

The Mental Clarity

Beyond physical health, detox can lead to enhanced mental clarity. The fog of lethargy that often accompanies a diet high in sugar and processed foods will start to lift. You may find it easier to concentrate and notice an improvement in memory and cognitive functions. This is a time when many experience a surge in creativity and productivity, finding joy in hobbies and activities they had previously set aside.

The Power of Support

Finally, seek support from friends, family, or a community of like-minded individuals embarking on their detox journeys. Sharing experiences, challenges, and successes can be incredibly motivating and will help you stay on course.

In conclusion, as you prepare to embark on this detox plan, brace yourself for a period of adjustment, but also look forward to the numerous benefits that await you on the other side. It's a process of transformation that will challenge you, yet also reward you in ways you might not have imagined. Keep your objectives in sight, stay committed, and most importantly, be patient and kind to yourself as you navigate through this phase.

11.2 Tips to Maximize Results

Tips to Maximize Results

Embarking on a detox plan, especially after the age of 50, is a brave decision that demonstrates a commitment to health and well-being. It's a pivotal moment where you choose to prioritize your body's needs, aiming for a more vibrant, active, and balanced life. This segment guides you through essential strategies to maximize your detox results, enabling you to harness the full potential of your commitment without sacrificing the joy of food and shared meals with loved ones.

Embrace a Whole Foods Mindset

The foundation of a successful detox lies in the quality of what you consume. Prioritizing whole, unprocessed foods is not just about removing toxins from your diet; it's about replenishing your body with the nutrients it needs to thrive. This shift towards foods in their most natural state—fruits, vegetables, lean proteins, and whole grains—ensures that every meal nourishes and supports your body's detoxification processes. The focus is on nutritional richness, where every bite contributes to your body's healing and revitalization.

Hydration: The Keystone of Detox

Water plays a non-negotiable role in your detox journey. It aids in flushing toxins from your system, keeps your cells hydrated, and supports optimal bodily functions. However, hydration extends beyond just water; it includes consuming foods with high water content and integrating herbal teas that complement the detox process. The goal is to consistently hydrate throughout the day, making it a habit rather than an afterthought. This continuous intake of fluids is crucial in facilitating the elimination of toxins and ensuring that your detox pathways are operating smoothly.

Mindful Eating: A Post-50 Philosophy

As we age, our relationship with food often requires reevaluation. Mindful eating becomes a powerful tool in maximizing detox results. It's about being present with your meals, savoring each bite, and listening to your body's signals. This practice helps in distinguishing between hunger and cravings, encouraging choices that align with your body's needs rather than impulsive desires. By slowing down and appreciating the flavors, textures, and sensations of your meals, you create a deep connection with food that transcends nutritional value, turning each meal into an opportunity for nourishment and gratitude.

Gentle Movement: Complementing Your Detox

Integrating movement into your detox plan enhances its effectiveness. Gentle exercises, such as walking, yoga, or stretching, support the body's natural detoxification processes by boosting circulation and lymphatic flow. This doesn't mean pushing your body to its limits; rather, it's about finding joy in movement and listening to your body's cues. Regular physical activity, tailored to your fitness level, complements the detox diet by facilitating toxin elimination and contributing to overall well-being.

Restorative Sleep: The Unsung Hero

Adequate rest is paramount in a detox plan. Sleep plays a critical role in the body's ability to heal, regenerate, and detoxify. Ensuring quality sleep each night supports the liver's detoxification cycles and helps regulate metabolism, contributing significantly to the detox process. Establishing a calming nighttime routine promotes better sleep patterns, making rest a priority ensures that your body has the optimal conditions for a successful detox.

Community and Support: Strength in Numbers

Lastly, don't underestimate the power of support. Whether it's family, friends, or an online community, sharing your detox journey can provide encouragement, share strategies, and celebrate milestones together. Surrounding yourself with positive influences keeps you motivated and accountable, making the path to a healthier lifestyle a collective, rather than solitary, endeavor.

In conclusion, following these strategies not only maximizes the results of your detox plan but also paves the way for lasting changes in your approach to health and wellness. By focusing on whole foods, staying hydrated, practicing mindful eating, integrating movement, prioritizing rest, and seeking support, you set the stage for a successful detox that reverberates well beyond the initial plan.

11.3 Shopping List and Meal Planning

Meal Planning Mastery

While having a comprehensive shopping list is important, the real secret to success lies in strategic meal planning. Meal planning ensures that you're not just eating randomly but consuming foods that synergistically work to support your detox and health goals. It also alleviates the daily stress of deciding what to eat, making it easier to stay on track.

<u>30-Day Meal Plans</u>

Day	Breakfast	Lunch	Dinner	Snack
1	Coconut Yogurt Parfait	Turmeric Chicken Salad	Grilled Salmon with Asparagus	Almond Butter and Banana Slices
2	Sweet Potato & Avocado Toast	Quinoa and Black Bean Salad	Chicken and Quinoa Salad	Avocado and Tomato Toast
3	Quinoa Veggie Breakfast Bowl	Ginger-Soy Salmon Fillets	Turmeric Cauliflower Steak	Greek Yogurt with Walnuts and Honey
4	Berry-Oat Smoothie Bowl	Kale and Avocado Wraps	Spinach and Salmon Stir-Fry	Cucumber and Hummus Cups
5	Spinach & Mushroom Omelet	Sweet Potato and Lentil Soup	Zucchini Noodles with Pesto	Berries and Almond Mix
6	Avocado Toast with Poached Egg	Lemon-Herb Baked Cod	Beetroot and Feta Salad	Spinach and Feta Stuffed Mushrooms
7	Spinach and Mint Smoothie	Chopped Veggie Bowl with Hummus	Ginger Tofu Stir-Fry	Turmeric and Honey Roasted Nuts
8	Quinoa and Cucumber Salad	Spiced Lentil Stew with Kale	Lemon Herb Grilled Chicken	Chia Seed Pudding
9	Oat and Banana Pancakes	Mediterranean Chickpea Salad	Roasted Pepper and Hummus Wrap	Smoked Salmon and Cucumber Rolls
10	Spinach and Mint Smoothie	Roasted Vegetable Quinoa Bowl	Coconut Curry Vegetable Stew	Kale Chips
11	Sweet Potato & Avocado Toast	Ginger-Soy Salmon Fillets	Turmeric Quinoa with Roasted Vegetables	Avocado and Tomato Toast
12	Quinoa Veggie Breakfast Bowl	Quinoa and Black Bean Salad	Avocado and Kale Salad	Almond Butter and Banana Slices

13	Berry-Oat Smoothie Bowl	Lemon-Herb Baked Cod	Chickpea and Sweet Potato Curry	Berries and Almond Mix
14	Coconut Yogurt Parfait	Sweet Potato and Lentil Soup	Lentil and Spinach Soup	Cucumber and Hummus Cups
15	Oat and Banana Pancakes	Spiced Lentil Stew with Kale	Zucchini Noodles with Pesto	Greek Yogurt with Walnuts and Honey
16	Spinach and Mint Smoothie	Turmeric Chicken Salad	Butternut Squash and Black Bean Enchiladas	Chia Seed Pudding
17	Avocado Toast with Poached Egg	Mediterranean Chickpea Salad	Cauliflower Steak with Herb Salsa	Smoked Salmon and Cucumber Rolls
18	Quinoa and Cucumber Salad	Chopped Veggie Bowl with Hummus	Vegan Mushroom Stroganoff	Turmeric and Honey Roasted Nuts
19	Berry-Oat Smoothie Bowl	Kale and Avocado Wraps	Beets and Quinoa Salad	Kale Chips
20	Spinach & Mushroom Omelet	Ginger-Soy Salmon Fillets	Spiced Apple Overnight Oats	Spinach and Feta Stuffed Mushrooms
21	Berry Protein Smoothie	Avocado Chicken Salad	Grilled Eggplant with Tomato Sauce	Pistachios and Dark Chocolate
22	Almond Butter Toast	Quinoa Tabbouleh	Vegan Chickpea Curry	Sliced Apples with Almond Butter
23	Mango Chia Pudding	Tomato Basil Soup	Zucchini Lasagna	Mixed Nuts and Dried Fruits
24	Oatmeal with Blueberries	Roasted Butternut Squash Salad	Lemon Garlic Tilapia	Carrot Sticks with Tahini Dip
25	Avocado and Egg Breakfast Wrap	Lentil Salad with Roasted Veggies	Stuffed Peppers	Greek Yogurt with Mixed Berries
26	Green Detox Smoothie	Spicy Black Bean Soup	Roasted Chicken and Vegetables	Guacamole with Veggie Chips
27	Scrambled Tofu on Toast	Caprese Salad with Balsamic Glaze	Vegetarian Paella	Cottage Cheese with Pineapple
28	Chia Seed and Berry Parfait	Chickpea and Avocado Wrap	Fish Tacos with Cabbage Slaw	Rice Cakes with Nut Butter
29	Vegan Banana Nut Muffins	Eggplant and Hummus Sandwich	Cauliflower Fried Rice	Dark Chocolate and Almonds
30	Pumpkin Spice Overnight Oats	Spicy Tuna Salad on Greens	Mushroom and Spinach Pasta	Pear Slices with Honey and Cheese

Chapter 12 :

The Week-by-Week Detox Plan

12.1 Focus on Purification

Focus on Purification

This first phase, entitled "Focus on Purification," is designed to cleanse your body, paving the way for a renewed internal environment. As you embark on this week, it's essential to understand that purification doesn't merely strip away what's unnecessary—it cultivates your body's resilience, improving its ability to manage blood sugar and enhance overall health.

Understanding Purification

At its core, purification is about reducing the intake of toxins and enhancing the body's capability to eliminate them. Toxins are substances that can cause negative health effects; they come from various sources including processed foods, environmental pollution, and even products we use daily. For individuals over 50, especially those managing diabetes, reducing toxin load is crucial as it can directly impact metabolic functions and insulin sensitivity.

The Process of Cleansing

This week, your diet will be meticulously curated to support liver function—your body's main detoxification organ. You'll incorporate foods rich in antioxidants and nutrients that promote cleansing and are known to be gentle on blood sugar levels. These include cruciferous vegetables like broccoli and Brussels sprouts, leafy greens such as kale and spinach, and other fibrous foods like legumes and whole grains.

The aim is not just to cleanse but to do so in a manner that respects and supports your body's nutritional needs, which can be quite specific after the age of 50. It's also important to consume adequate amounts of lean protein sources like fish or chicken, as protein is essential for the repair and growth of tissues.

Hydration: The Unsung Hero

One of the pillars of effective detoxification is hydration. Water is not just a thirst-quencher—it is vital for transporting nutrients to your cells, helping with digestion, and flushing toxins from your body. Aim to drink at least eight glasses of water daily, as proper hydration aids in kidney function and ensures that toxins are efficiently removed through urine.

Herbal Teas and Their Role

Incorporating certain herbal teas can be beneficial in enhancing your body's detox processes. Teas like dandelion or milk thistle are known for their liver-supportive properties. They can help increase the production of bile, assisting in the elimination of toxins from the body. However, ensure any herbal intake is in moderation and consult your healthcare provider, especially when managing diabetes, to avoid any adverse effects with medications.

Rest and Digestive Health

Adequate sleep is another cornerstone of the purification week. Sleep gives your body the needed time to repair and reorganize. During sleep, your brain signals the body to release hormones that encourage tissue growth and repair blood vessels, aiding in the detoxification processes and helping manage blood glucose levels more effectively.

Good digestive health is equally paramount. A well-functioning digestive system ensures that toxins are efficiently processed and expelled. Foods rich in fiber play an essential role here as they help regulate the body's use of sugars, helping to keep hunger and blood glucose in check.

Emotional Cleansing

Lastly, it's not just your physical being that requires cleansing. Emotional health has a profound impact on physical health, especially for those managing chronic conditions like diabetes. This week, take the opportunity to engage in activities that reduce stress, such as meditation, yoga, or simply spending time in nature. Managing stress is crucial as it can directly affect glucose levels and overall wellbeing.

As you follow the Focus on Purification, remember that this is just the beginning. You're setting up your body to succeed in the next phases of your detox plan. This week is about creating a cleaner, more efficient internal environment, enabling you to tackle the next steps with vigor and resilience. Remember, the goal is not to rush through this purification process but to embrace it as a fundamental and rejuvenating phase in your journey toward a healthier lifestyle.

12.2 Restoring Balance

Restoring Balance

Embarking on the path to restoring balance, especially for those over 50 living with diabetes, is about reharmonizing the body's natural rhythms and systems. This phase is crucial, as it's where you begin to truly feel the transformation set forth by your efforts in purification. Your goal here isn't merely to adjust your diet but to cultivate a lifestyle that sustains your health, happiness, and blood sugar levels in harmony. This approach pivots on understanding the delicate interplay between nutrition, physical activity, and stress management, adjusted to the unique needs of your body after 50.

Nutritional Harmony

At the heart of restoring balance is fine-tuning your diet to nourish your body without spiking your blood sugar levels. Now that your body is primed for renewal, it's time to introduce a wider variety of foods back into your diet. The focus should remain on whole, nutrient-dense foods that support blood sugar regulation and provide the vitality necessary for a full life.

The cornerstone of your meals should be balance—between protein, fats, and carbohydrates. Emphasizing low-glycemic index (GI) carbohydrates from vegetables, fruits, and whole grains will help stabilize blood sugar levels. These choices not only provide essential nutrients and fiber but also aid in satiety, helping prevent overeating. Pairing these with lean proteins and healthy fats in each meal further assists in maintaining blood sugar and energy levels throughout the day.

Incorporating diverse protein sources, such as fish rich in omega-3 fatty acids, lean poultry, legumes, and nuts, supports tissue repair and muscle maintenance, which naturally decline with age. Likewise, healthy fats from avocados, olive oil, and nuts are not just good for the heart; they play a pivotal role in absorbing fat-soluble vitamins and antioxidants, crucial for combating inflammation and supporting overall health.

Physical Engagement

Balance extends beyond what you eat. Integrating regular, moderate physical activity into your routine is pivotal. Exercise, be it brisk walking, swimming, or yoga, does more than burn calories. It enhances insulin sensitivity, making your body more efficient at managing blood sugar levels. Moreover, physical activity stimulates endorphins, the body's natural mood elevators, which can help alleviate stress and foster a positive outlook on life.

Building a routine that's both enjoyable and sustainable is key. Activities shared with friends or family not only contribute to your physical well-being but also strengthen social bonds, enhancing emotional health.

Stress Management and Quality of Life

Managing stress is not just about feeling less harried; it's about creating an environment in which your body can thrive. Chronic stress has a direct impact on blood glucose levels, making stress management a critical component of restoring balance. Techniques such as deep breathing, meditation, or even engaging in hobbies can significantly reduce stress levels, helping mitigate its impact on your diabetes.

Quality sleep is another vital element in this equation. Sleep is a time for the body to repair itself, and disturbances in sleep can affect blood sugar control. Establishing a soothing nightly routine and ensuring 7-8 hours of restful sleep can have profound effects on your well-being.

Emotional Well-being

Lastly, pay attention to your emotional health. Living with diabetes, especially later in life, can sometimes feel daunting. However, adopting a positive mindset and approach towards managing your condition can transform this challenge into a journey of self-discovery and empowerment. Actively seeking support from loved ones or groups with similar challenges can provide encouragement, understanding, and practical advice, making the journey less isolating.

12.3 Strengthening the Immune System

At this juncture of our detox adventure, our attention shifts to a vitally crucial frontier - amplifying the fortitude of your immune system. With the purification process setting the stage and balance being adeptly restored, fortifying your immune defenses becomes the protagonist in the narrative of your health overhaul.

As the exemplary individual over 50, resolute in managing diabetes while reveling in the culinary delights and social rituals of food, you understand the importance of a stout immune system. You recognize it as your body's esteemed sentinel, unceasingly vigilant against external threats that could jeopardize your well-being and exacerbate diabetic complications.

In a world teeming with pathogens and daily stressors, a robust immune response is your ally in minimizing illnesses that can derail your determined efforts and active lifestyle. How we enhance this line of defense is through a strategic confluence of diet, exercise, and stress-reducing practices.

A Nourished Immune Army

Our immune system thrives on a myriad of nutrients that boost its function. Seize every meal as an occasion to incorporate a rich tapestry of vitamins, minerals, and antioxidants – the chivalrous knights in your body's ongoing battle for health.

Begin with vibrantly colored vegetables and fruits, the stalwarts loaded with vitamin C, vitamin E, beta-carotene, and phytonutrients. These are the masterful craftspeople bolstering the assembly of your immune cells. They work concurrently with minerals such as zinc, found in seeds and legumes, and selenium, present in nuts, notably the Brazil nut – each a cog in the intricate gearing of the immune machinery.

Proteins, the very building blocks of your muscles and antibodies, must grace each plate. Lean meats, tofu, and lentils are substantial sources. Alongside these, fatty fish like salmon and mackerel provide omega-3 fatty acids. These not only cool the fires of inflammation but are wizards in the art of immunomodulation.

And let's not forget the unsung heroes – probiotics. Fermented foods such as yogurt, kefir, and sauerkraut house these friendly bacteria that serve as sentinels within your gut. They not only guard crucial terrain where many immune interactions take place but also communicate signals to the rest of the immune battalion.

With the ensemble of these nutritional allies, each meal becomes an opportunity tostify your immune forces, enhancing your ability to thwart infections and remain in control of your diabetes management.

Sweat and Strength for Immune Resilience

We pivot now to physical exertion – a catalyst for immune invigoration. Moderate, consistent exercise is the master key to unlocking an active and resilient immune response. It elevates our natural killer cells and circulates them more readily, on patrol and prepared to tackle intruding pathogens.

Walking briskly under the nurturing caress of the sun bestows upon you not only cardiovascular stamina but also precious vitamin D, which plays a decisive role in immune function. Swimming and cycling, embraced with equal fervor, ensure that your legions of immune cells are ever-vigilant and effective.

Engage in routines that respect your body's pace, relish in movements that bring you joy, and establish a rhythm that you can persist in. Physical vitality perpetuates immune might.

An Empowered Steward of your Health

Through the diligent application of these practices – refining your diet, instilling a non-negotiable commitment to physical activity, and mastering the subtle art of stress management – you are not merely following a week-by-week plan. You are laying down the cobblestones of a resilient life path.

A triumphant immune system, aligned with meticulous diabetic control, gifts you the authority to reign over your health, ensuring you can bask in the precious moments with family and friends for years to come. Cherish and harness this newfound strength, for it is your unwavering shield against life's uncertainties.

In essence, strengthening your immune.

12.4 Maintenance and Preventing Relapses

The Foundation of Sustained Success

Sustaining your health transformation requires more than just understanding what to eat and what to avoid; it involves establishing a solid foundation. This foundation is built upon the principles of mindful eating, consistent activity, and regular monitoring of your health.

Mindful eating is about connecting more deeply with your food. It's appreciating the flavors, textures, and nutrients that each meal provides. This practice helps you recognize when you are truly hungry and when you are eating for other reasons such as stress or boredom. Embedding mindfulness into your eating routine can be as simple as taking five deep breaths before each meal to center yourself or chewing slowly and deliberately to savor each bite.

Physical activity should be integrated into your daily life as a non-negotiable component. Find activities that you enjoy and can look forward to, whether it's a morning swim, an evening walk, or a dance class with friends. The aim is to keep your body moving, your blood flowing, and your glucose levels stable.

Regular monitoring involves keeping a close eye on your blood sugar levels, understanding how different foods and activities impact your readings, and adjusting as necessary. It's about becoming an expert on your own body and its responses. Regular check-ins with healthcare professionals can also provide you with additional insights and adjustments to your routine.

Creating a Supportive Environment

Your environment plays a significant role in your long-term success. This includes your physical surroundings, the food readily available to you, and your social circle. Consider making your home a sanctuary for your health goals. Stock your kitchen with nutritious foods that support your diabetic diet and create an inviting space for physical activity that inspires regular use.

Your social circle can offer emotional support, motivation, and accountability. Sharing your goals with friends and family can help them understand how best to support you. You might even inspire them to join you in healthier habits.

Embracing Flexibility and Compassion

Despite our best efforts, there may be times when we face setbacks or make choices that don't align with our health goals. It's crucial to approach these moments with a sense of flexibility and self-compassion, rather than harsh self-judgment. Understanding that perfection is not the goal, but rather consistent improvement, can prevent a temporary slip from turning into a significant relapse. Learn from these experiences and use them to strengthen your resolve.

Chapter 13 :

Beyond Diet - A Comprehensive Lifestyle

13.1 Integrating Movement into Your Daily Routine

As we advance beyond the age of 50, the journey toward maintaining a healthy and balanced lifestyle becomes increasingly intertwined with our everyday choices. Among these, integrating movement into our daily routine emerges as a crucial, yet often overlooked aspect. This is especially true for individuals managing diabetes, where consistent physical activity can significantly influence blood sugar control, heart health, and overall well-being.

The Foundation of Daily Movement

Understanding the importance of movement in our daily lives goes beyond mere exercise. It's about creating a lifestyle that embraces physical activity as a natural part of our day, not an obligation. The integration of movement can transform not just our physical health but our mental state, influencing how we engage with ourselves and the world around us.

For those over 50 with diabetes, the stakes are even higher. Regular physical activity can improve insulin sensitivity, help in managing weight, and reduce the risks associated with cardiovascular diseases. Yet, the approach should not be daunting but rather a seamless addition to one's lifestyle.

Creating Opportunities for Movement

The key to integrating movement lies in recognizing and creating opportunities within your existing daily routine. This could mean choosing to take the stairs instead of the elevator, parking a little further from the grocery store entrance, or even engaging in light stretching while watching television. Small, deliberate choices add up, creating a fabric of physical activity that supports your health goals.

Engaging in household chores can also be a source of movement. Gardening, vacuuming, or simply moving around while tidying up can keep your body active and contribute to your daily movement goals. The beauty of these activities is their dual purpose; accomplishing necessary tasks while also benefiting your health.

Walking: The Underestimated Exercise

Walking embodies the perfect exercise for any age but holds particular value for those in their golden years. It's accessible, simple, and can be tailored to fit any fitness level. A daily walk, whether it be a brisk morning jaunt or a leisurely evening stroll, can do wonders for your physical and mental health. It's an opportunity to reflect, unwind, or connect with nature and your community. Gradually increasing the duration or pace can also subtly enhance your physical endurance without the strain of high-impact exercises.

Incorporating Structured Activities

While spontaneous movement is beneficial, incorporating structured physical activities can provide focused benefits. This might include yoga, Pilates, or tai chi classes designed to improve flexibility, balance, and muscle strength, all areas of concern as we age. Additionally, these settings offer social interaction, which can further motivate and uplift your spirits.

Water aerobics or swimming are other excellent activities, particularly for those seeking low-impact options. The buoyancy of water reduces stress on joints, making it easier to perform exercises that might otherwise be challenging.

The Role of Technology

In today's digital age, technology offers various tools to assist in integrating movement into your daily life. Fitness trackers and smartphone apps can monitor physical activity, set daily goals, and offer reminders to keep moving. They serve not only as a motivational tool but also as a means to tangibly measure your progress.

Reflection and Adjustment

As with any lifestyle change, integrating movement into your routine requires reflection and adjustment. It's important to listen to your body and respect its limits. If an activity causes discomfort, exploring alternatives is both wise and necessary. The goal is not to push through pain but to find joy in the movement.

Conclusion

Incorporating movement into your daily routine is about finding balance and joy in activity. It's an acknowledgment that every bit of movement counts towards your larger goal of a healthy, active lifestyle. This chapter encourages you to view physical activity not as a separate task but as an inherent part of your day. The shift from seeing exercise as optional to essential can profoundly impact your health journey, particularly in managing diabetes after the age of 50. By embracing movement in all its forms, you equip yourself with a powerful tool in maintaining health, vitality, and independence.

13.2 Stress Management and Mental Wellbeing

The Undeniable Connection to Your Health

When you reach a certain milestone in life say post-50 priorities shift. Among the myriad concerns, managing diabetes surfaces as a paramount challenge. But here's something crucial to ponder: How often do we consider the silent undercurrents of stress and its impact on our mental wellbeing, especially as it intertwines with diabetes management? This chapter aims to unpack the potent synergy between stress management and mental wellbeing, and its non-negotiable role in managing diabetes after 50.

The Unseen Battle: Stress and Its Metabolic Blowback

In the landscape of our lives, stress is an omnipresent shadow, creeping in through crevices left unguarded. For those navigating the complexities of diabetes, stress isn't merely an emotional inconvenience; it's a direct antagonist to blood glucose control. The physiological chain reaction sparking from stress to elevated blood glucose levels is a testament to the mind-body symphony, playing a tune we can't afford to ignore.

Why, you might wonder, does this matter more after 50? The tapestry of life post-50 is often woven with finer threads retirement considerations, adult children, aging parents, and, for many, the stark reality of managing chronic conditions like diabetes. Each of these factors can harbor stress, creating a feedback loop that directly impacts glycemic control.

Crafting Your Calm: Tools for Tranquility

In the arsenal against stress, your strongest weapons are often the simplest. The art of mindfulness meditation is one such ally. Stripping away the complexities of life, it invites you to anchor in the now, training your mind to dwell less on the stress triggers and more on the moment. Regular practice dims the stress signals, allowing for a serene mental environment conducive to managing diabetcs.

Then there's the breath your constant companion, yet often an overlooked tool. Deep-breathing exercises serve as a bridge to tranquility, guiding your nervous system back to a restorative calm. This biological reset button can be a cornerstone of stress management, buffering you against the glucose-elevating storms of life's stresses.

Joy and Connection: The Rhythms of Resilience

Engaging in activities that spark joy is not just a frivolous pursuit; it's a cornerstone of mental wellbeing. Whether it's the creative expression found in painting, the rhythmic strumming of a guitar, or the simple act of tending to a garden, these endeavors offer a sanctuary from stress. They invite a state of flow of being so absorbed in an activity that time and worries fade into the background. This consequential lowering of stress levels can directly influence blood glucose management, offering a pleasant reprieve in the daily dance with diabetes.

Moreover, the strength of social connections cannot be understated. Isolation breeds stress; community fosters resilience. In the fabric of your post-50 life, weaving strong social threads be it through family, friends, or diabetes support groups can create a resilient network. These connections offer not just an emotional outlet but a sharing of experiences, tips, and encouragement vital for navigating diabetes.

Professional Guidance: A Beacon in the Storm

Recognizing when stress has tipped into the realm of the unmanageable is crucial. There's profound strength in seeking professional help ,a counselor or therapist equipped to navigate the emotional byways can be an invaluable guide. They can provide tailored strategies for de-escalating stress, offering not just a roadmap to better mental wellbeing but also a companion in your journey toward optimal diabetes management.

The Road Ahead

The complex interplay between stress, mental wellbeing, and diabetes demands a comprehensive approach, one that acknowledges the power of the mind over the body. By prioritizing stress reduction and mental health, you're not just aiming for better diabetes control; you're championing a life filled with more joy, resilience, and connection. This isn't just about managing diabetes; it's about redefining the quality of your life in its most enriching chapters.

13.3 Restorative Sleep for Better Glycemic Control

In the pursuit of managing diabetes after the age of 50, much emphasis is placed on diet and exercise. While these elements are foundational to controlling your blood glucose levels, there's another pillar of health that often doesn't receive the attention it deserves: restorative sleep. For individuals striving to maintain a balanced lifestyle that keeps diabetes in check without sacrificing the joy of food or the company of others, understanding the profound impact of sleep on glycemic control is essential.

The Underrated Power of Sleep

Sleep, especially restorative sleep, plays a crucial role in managing diabetes. It's during these deep periods of rest that our bodies undergo critical processes of repair and recovery. For people over 50, achieving consistent, high-quality sleep can directly influence how effectively the body regulates blood sugar levels. Insufficient or poor-quality sleep disrupts the body's insulin sensitivity, a condition where your body does not use insulin as efficiently as it should. This can lead to higher blood glucose levels, making diabetes more difficult to manage.

Moreover, a lack of restorative sleep can escalate stress hormones in the body, such as cortisol, which further exacerbates blood sugar control issues. When these hormones flood your system, they can cause your blood sugar levels to spike, pushing your diligent dietary efforts to the sidelines. Combating this begins with understanding the importance of, and actively pursuing, better sleep patterns.

Strategies for Enhancing Sleep Quality

Enhancing sleep quality is a multi-faceted approach that requires adjustments to both daytime and nighttime routines. Engaging in regular physical activity during the day can significantly improve the quality of your sleep. Exercise not only helps tire the body in a natural, healthy way, but it also helps regulate your circadian rhythm, the body's internal clock that signals when it's time to sleep or wake up.

Creating a bedtime routine is equally important. This routine might include winding down for 30 minutes before sleep, avoiding screens and bright lights, and engaging in calming activities such as reading or meditation. The goal is to signal to your body that it's time to shift into sleep mode, preparing you for a restorative night's sleep.

Additionally, pay attention to your sleep environment. The ideal sleeping environment is cool, dark, and quiet. Consider investing in blackout curtains, using white noise machines, and ensuring your mattress and pillows support a comfortable night's sleep.

Navigating Sleep Challenges with Age

As we age, we often face new challenges that can impact our sleep, such as increased frequency of waking up during the night and a shift in sleep patterns that may cause us to become tired earlier. However, these changes don't have to spell disaster for your glycemic control. Adapting your sleep habits, such as ensuring you still get 7 to 8 hours of sleep by adjusting your bedtime or incorporating a nap during the day, can help manage these shifts. Remaining flexible and attentive to your body's needs is paramount in maintaining restorative sleep patterns.

Maintaining a consistent sleep schedule is also vital. Going to bed and waking up at the same time every day, including weekends, can significantly improve your sleep quality. This consistency helps regulate your body's internal clock and can aid in falling asleep and staying asleep through the night.

Intertwining Sleep with Lifestyle Management

In the tapestry of diabetes management, sleep intertwines with diet and physical activity, each impacting the others. The relationship between them is symbiotic; improving one aspect can lead to benefits in another. For instance, a diet rich in nutrients and low in sugars and simple carbohydrates can improve sleep quality, just as regular physical activity can. In turn, achieving restorative sleep can provide you with more energy for physical activities and can enhance your body's insulin sensitivity, making dietary management more effective.

In essence, restorative sleep is not a luxury but a necessity for those managing diabetes post-50. It's a powerful tool in your arsenal for maintaining blood glucose levels, preventing complications, and enhancing overall wellbeing.

Chapter 14 :

Additional Resources

14.1 FAQs About the Diabetic Diet for Those Over 50

Navigating dietary choices can be particularly challenging as we age, especially when managing conditions like diabetes. This section addresses common questions that surface when those over 50 adapt their diets to better manage their diabetes, helping you feel empowered and knowledgeable without compromising the joy of eating and sharing meals with loved ones.

Why is diet so crucial for managing diabetes after 50?

Post 50, your body undergoes significant changes that can affect how it processes glucose. Muscle mass typically decreases, which affects how your body uses sugar, potentially increasing blood glucose levels if not managed properly. A well-considered diabetic diet helps to mitigate these changes by maintaining healthy blood sugar levels, which is crucial in reducing the risk of diabetes-related complications such as neuropathy, retinopathy, and heart disease.

What are the key components of an effective diabetic diet for those over 50?

The cornerstone of a diabetes-friendly diet after 50 isn't dramatically different from the basic principles of healthy eating. However, emphasis is placed on controlling portions, choosing whole foods over processed ones, staying hydrated, and balancing the intake of carbs, proteins, and fats. The objective is to stabilize blood sugar levels while considering the natural metabolic deceleration and insulin sensitivity changes that occur with age.

Can dietary changes alone manage my diabetes effectively?

Diet is fundamental in managing diabetes, but it's most effective when paired with other lifestyle adjustments. Regular physical activity, adequate restorative sleep, and stress management all play vital roles in controlling blood glucose levels. For some, medication may also be necessary to maintain proper glycemic control. Always consult with your healthcare provider to tailor a comprehensive approach that fits your health status and lifestyle needs.

How can I adapt favorite recipes to be more diabetes-friendly?

Recreating your favorite dishes to fit a diabetes-friendly profile can be both satisfying and a creative challenge. Start by reducing simple carbohydrates and sugars; for instance, replace white rice with quinoa or cauliflower rice. Increase the fiber content in meals by adding more vegetables and whole grains which can help to slow the rise in blood glucose levels after eating. Consider using spices and fresh herbs instead of salt to enhance flavor without added health risks.

Are sugar substitutes safe and effective for those over 50 with diabetes?

Artificial sweeteners and sugar substitutes can be a contentious topic. While they do offer a way to enjoy sweetness without the direct glucose spike, some studies suggest that they might influence your body's ability to regulate blood sugar effectively or impact gut health. Natural sweeteners like stevia or monk fruit provide an alternative but use them sparingly. It's best to cultivate a taste for less sweetness to effectively manage diabetes.

What types of foods should I focus on to ensure a balanced diet?

Incorporating a variety of nutrient-dense foods is vital. Lean proteins such as chicken, turkey, and fish, alongside beans and lentils, are excellent sources. Include a wealth of colorful fruits and vegetables to ensure you're getting enough vitamins and minerals. Whole grains should replace refined carbohydrates, and healthy fats from avocados, nuts, seeds, or olive oil should be used to cook and prepare meals.

What should I do if I experience blood sugar spikes or dips?

First, understand the foods or activities that cause these fluctuations. Keep a food and symptom diary to track your responses. If you're experiencing frequent spikes or dips, it might be necessary to adjust your meal composition or timing. Consult with your healthcare provider to discuss these patterns and potentially adapt your medication or management plan.

Approaching your dietary management of diabetes with knowledge, adaptability, and proactive measures allows you not only to live healthily but to enjoy the richness of well-prepared nourishing meals.

14.2 Extra Tips for Maintaining Long-term Motivation

Maintaining long-term motivation in managing diabetes through a healthy diet isn't just about strict adherence to dietary guidelines; it's about embracing a lifestyle change that celebrates the essence of living fully, even with diabetes. This chapter symbolizes not just a phase in your life but the beginning of an enriching path toward well-being and autonomy.

Understanding the Why

Initially, let's address the 'why.' This critical question serves as the foundation of your motivation. You aim to live a vibrant, healthy life, free from the burdens diabetes can impose. Remember, you're not merely following a diet; you're building a fortress for your health, ensuring you're present and robust for the adventures and moments that matter most with your friends and family.

Simplifying the How

The prospect of transforming your diet can be daunting. However, breaking it down into achievable, simple steps is vital. Start with small, manageable changes like introducing one diabetes-friendly recipe a week or replacing sugar-sweetened beverages with water and unsweetened teas. These small victories build momentum, making the transition less overwhelming and more manageable.

Celebrating Every Victory

Each step you successfully take towards your dietary goals is a victory worth celebrating. It could be as minor as choosing salad over fries or as major as your first month without refined sugar. Acknowledge and revel in these accomplishments. They are tangible proof of your commitment to your health and the progress you're making.

The Role of Support

No one should navigate their health journey in isolation. Engaging family and friends, sharing your goals, and even inviting them to join you in your dietary changes can provide an invaluable source of encouragement. Additionally, participating in community groups, either in-person or online, aligns you with others on similar paths, offering mutual support and inspiration.

Embrace Flexibility

Life is unpredictable, and there will be times when sticking strictly to your diet isn't feasible. During holidays, vacations, or special occasions, give yourself permission to enjoy without guilt. The key is balance and returning to your dietary plan without despair or self-reprimand. This flexibility can maintain long-term motivation by preventing feelings of deprivation and frustration.

Educating Yourself

Knowledge is power. Understanding the impact of diabetes and how your diet influences your health can reinforce your motivation. As you learn more about the nutritional value of foods and the physiologic bases of diabetes management, your dietary choices become more informed, fostering a sense of empowerment and control over your health trajectory.

Setting Realistic Expectations

Progress, not perfection, is the aim. Setting unrealistic expectations can lead to disappointment and a sense of inadequacy, undermining your motivation. Understanding that there will be ups and downs, recognizing your progress over perfection, reinforces a sustainable, long-term commitment to dietary management.

Reframing Your Perspective

Instead of viewing diet as a restriction, see it as an exploration of culinary diversity. Discovering new foods, recipes, and preparation methods can transform the dietary management of diabetes into an exciting adventure in flavors and nourishment, rather than a monotonous regimen.

Journey Journaling

Documenting your journey can be a powerful motivator. Keep a journal to reflect on your daily achievements, thoughts, and feelings about your progress. During challenging times, reflecting on your journey and witnessing how far you've come can reignite your motivation.

Prioritizing Self-compassion

Lastly, and perhaps most importantly, is self-compassion. There will be days when you feel you've veered off course. Instead of self-criticism, offer yourself compassion and understanding, just as you would a friend. Remind yourself why you're on this journey and the life you envision living as a result. This kindness and patience with oneself can be the most significant motivator in times of struggle.

In essence, maintaining long-term motivation in managing diabetes with diet is a multifaceted endeavor that transcends mere food choices. It's about cultivating an enriching lifestyle that embraces health, support, flexibility, and self-compassion. It's a commitment to living your best life, nourishing not just your body but also your spirit and relationships, turning dietary management into a rewarding path toward wellness and vitality.

14.3 Form to Request a Personal Medical Consultation

Navigating through life after the age of fifty with diabetes introduces not just a set of challenges but a realm of opportunities to redefine one's relationship with food and overall well-being. The shift towards seeking a healthier, more balanced lifestyle, especially concerning one's diet, is not just about managing blood sugar levels. It's about reclaiming joy, pleasure, and independence in one's life, sharing memorable meals with family and friends, and stepping away from the shadow of potential health complications that loom over uncontrolled glycemic levels.

Understanding the vital role of personalized medical consultation cannot be overstated. It's a step beyond reading books and assimilating information; it's about tailoring that knowledge to fit your unique health profile. This is where the Form to Request a Personal Medical Consultation becomes an indispensable tool in one's arsenal, serving as a direct line of communication between you and your healthcare provider. It is essential in ensuring that the advice and strategies developed are not only effective but also sustainable and enjoyable for you.

A personal medical consultation goes beyond a mere clinical interaction. It's an engagement that recognizes you as a whole person, with unique tastes, preferences, and lifestyle. It's about building a partnership with your healthcare provider, where your voice, concerns, and goals are central to the conversation. This consultation is aimed at crafting a dietary plan that is not only medically sound but also aligned with your individual needs and circumstances, ensuring that the measures you take genuinely enhance your quality of life.

In this consultation, your healthcare provider will delve into various aspects critical to formulating a comprehensive and effective dietary strategy tailored to managing diabetes post fifty. They will consider your medical history, current health status, and dietary habits. They will also take into account your physical activity levels, living arrangements, and any other factors that might influence your dietary needs and goals. This holistic approach ensures that the recommendations made are not only aimed at controlling blood sugar levels but also at promoting overall health and wellness.

Moreover, this consultation is an opportunity to address concerns and questions in a supportive and informative environment. It's a chance to dispel myths, clarify doubts, and gain a deeper understanding of how different foods and lifestyle choices affect your diabetes management. This conversation can cover a range of topics from the specifics of carbohydrate counting to the impact of stress on blood sugar levels, providing you with a wealth of knowledge to make informed decisions daily.

The goal of this consultation is empowerment. By the end of it, you should feel confident in your ability to make healthy dietary choices that don't compromise on flavor or satisfaction. Your healthcare provider will equip you with practical strategies, tips, and potentially even meal plans that reflect your tastes and preferences while keeping your diabetes management on track. This tailored approach ensures that you can still enjoy the foods you love, share meals with family and friends, and lead an active, independent life, all while maintaining effective control over your diabetes.

By initiating this consultation, you are affirming your commitment to a future where diabetes management and dietary satisfaction go hand in hand, paving the way for a healthier, happier you.

Conclusion

As we draw the curtains on this comprehensive journey through the terrain of diabetes management and the path to a balanced, fulfilling diet post fifty, I want to take a moment to acknowledge the steps you've taken simply by engaging with this material. By sharing this journey with you, my aim has been not only to illuminate the possibilities that a mindful and deliberate approach to eating can offer but also to demonstrate that managing diabetes in the later stages of life can be a fulfilling adventure rather than a restrictive burden.

The essence of everything we've explored together in this book isn't just about categorizing foods as 'good' or 'bad', nor is it solely about the biochemical impacts of what we eat. At its heart, it's about revisiting our relationship with food and, by extension, with ourselves and our bodies as we age. This endeavor is fundamentally a celebration of life and the myriad ways through which we can continue to enjoy it, despite the challenges posed by diabetes.

Managing diabetes after fifty requires a nuanced understanding of not only our bodies and how they interact with food but also the emotional and social dimensions of eating and sharing meals. It's a balance that recognizes the pleasure that food can bring into our lives and the role it plays in bringing us together with those we care about. It's about finding joy in the textures, flavors, and colors of our meals, and the joy of living a life not defined by restrictions, but empowered by choices.

Throughout this book, we've navigated the technicalities of managing blood sugar, the principles of a diet that supports your health goals, and the psychological aspects of making sustainable changes. These are not just chapters in a book but chapters in your life, each marking a step towards a more aware, healthier, and balanced existence.

Remember, managing diabetes is not a solitary journey. It's a path you walk with the support of your healthcare providers, your family, your friends, and a community of individuals who share similar experiences and aspirations. The Form to Request a Personal Medical Consultation, which we discussed, is a tool, a starting point for deepening the dialogue between you and your healthcare team, ensuring that your approach to managing diabetes is as individualized and effective as possible.

As you continue to navigate your way through the thrills and challenges of managing diabetes, let this book serve not only as a guide but also as a companion. The stories of success shared here are a testament to what is possible when you approach your health goals with determination, optimism, and a willingness to adapt and learn.

In the end, the message I want to leave you with is one of hope and empowerment. Diabetes, particularly in the later stages of life, presents unique challenges, but it also presents unique opportunities - to reconnect with your body, to rediscover the joys of cooking and eating, and to redefine what it means to live healthily. The lifestyle changes we've discussed are not just about diabetes; they're about taking control of your health and your life in a way that brings you joy, satisfaction, and well-being.

My sincerest hope is that the information, strategies, and stories contained in these pages will inspire you to embrace the challenges and opportunities of managing diabetes with grace and joy. Here's to your health, your happiness, and your continued journey towards a balanced, vibrant life.

Warmest regards,

Dr. Madison Wells

Made in the USA
Columbia, SC
18 July 2024

38965989R00057